BODY LANGUAGE

THIS IS A CARLTON BOOK

Text copyright © 1995 Carlton Books Limited
Design and illustration copyright © 2004
Carlton Books Limited

This updated and revised edition published by
Carlton Books Limited 2004
20 Mortimer Street
London W1T 3JW

A CIP catalogue record for this book is available
from the British Library.

ISBN 1 84442 675 0

Printed and bound in Dubai

Executive Editor: Lisa Dyer
Design: Zoë Dissell
Copy Editors: Jonathan Hilton and
    Lara Maiklem
Production Controller: Caroline Alberti

Illustrations by Robin Max Marder

BODY LANGUAGE

Actions speak louder than words: crack the **unspoken code** of body language

SUSAN QUILLIAM

CARLTON BOOKS

contents

introduction
page 6

office life
page 82

4

The body language of
the workplace

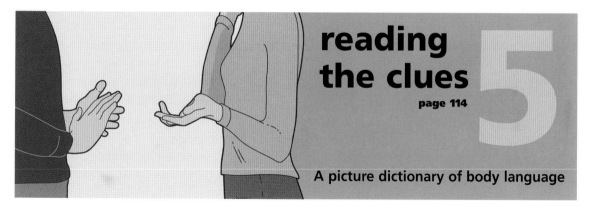

reading
the clues
page 114

5

A picture dictionary of body language

introduction

Body language has always fascinated human beings. We have always wanted to understand the message behind the words; we have always wanted to know what people really mean by a glance, a blush, a gesture.

Now we've realized that we cannot only use body language to interpret other people's actions, we can also use it to give ourselves increased effectiveness in life. Now, body talk can help us succeed in life, in love, at work.

Humans have probably always known instinctively that our non-verbal communication is just as vital as our verbal communication. How many of us were told when young to 'pull ourselves up straight' because our parents realized that would make us look more intelligent, attractive or impressive. And now, research has shown that if we alter the way we present ourselves to the world – with friends, at work, in love – we stand a much greater chance of success.

This book explains how to improve your body language and the specially commissioned illustrations show you what works and what doesn't. It encourages you to analyze and interpret others' bodytalk so that you can tell in advance how to respond to them, then adapt your own bodytalk for maximum impact.

Speechless

This first chapter of the book explains what body language is and how to use it. It also includes the basic 'vocabulary' you need in order to read the book, and introduces the vital signs and essential guidelines for using body language in your life.

Face to face

Through reading non-verbal signs you can be extremely accurate in analyzing what people are thinking and feeling, even in reading their personality. How can you use body language to make initial contact with someone? How can you build friendship – and how can you tell when friendship is fading? How can you make impact socially, at parties, in small and large groups?

This chapter also explores different kinds of relationships you can have with others, personal and professional; how to get time alone and how to respect other people's need for solitude through your own body language; and finally, how to use body language to survive in public.

Love signs

The body language of intimate relationships is explored in chapter three, first looking at what draws people to each other and how you can use this knowledge to create and build attraction. How can you move a relationship forward, both sexually by using passionate body language, and emotionally by understanding your partner and communicating your feelings to him or her?

This chapter looks at relationship problems and how body language can be used to trouble-shoot. What happens when you argue? Is it possible to tell if a partner is having an affair? How can you use body language to develop a more honest relationship? What are the signals of a committed and long-term partnership?

Office life

Chapter four takes non-verbal communication into the workplace. Coping with colleagues, making friends, maintaining status, and surviving workplace affairs are all covered, as well as management issues – how to handle your boss, then how to cope when you become a boss yourself. Also discussed are interview tactics, and – once you've gained your promotion – how to use body language to lead your team.

Reading the clues

The final section of the book is a visual dictionary of body language. The illustrations show signals, movements and expressions and the text provides interpretations. One expression or gesture can mean many different things – it is only when bodytalk is read in context that you can really interpret it accurately.

How to use the book

This book is designed so that you can read it from cover to cover, and so get a comprehensive over-view of what body language can do. But you can also dip into it, reading different sections in order to guide you through a particular situation such an interview, a party, a date. If you do this, however, be sure to read chapter one first, as it gives you some basic ground rules for using body language. Study the pictures as well as the words. The captions can never tell the whole story though; look at the illustrations again for yourself, and try interpreting every signal in them, not just the ones the text refers to.

Finally, use the book as a starting point, adding to it from your own experience and learning what works for you and what doesn't. When it comes to bodytalk, given knowledge and practise, you can be your own expert.

1 speechless

If your aim is to get the most out of life, then what you need is 'bodytalk'. The study of body language – the art of non-verbal communication – is possibly the most exciting and useful development in personal psychology today, adding a whole new dimension to what you can understand about people and a whole new set of possibilities as to what you can achieve in the world.

How the body communicates

Human beings use many different channels of communication. Yet, despite thousands of years of human development, we have regarded only the verbal channels as important – what we say and what we write. It's only during the last 40 years or so that we've realized that there's an entire channel – non-verbal communication – which is just as important as words, because it gives us just as much, if not more, information about what people are thinking and feeling. Some estimates reckon that up to 93 per cent of the information we receive about any situation comes non-verbally rather than verbally. So, whenever you chat with a friend, ask your boss for a pay rise, or set out to seduce, what you do may be up to 13 times as information-packed as what you say.

Mind-reading

Body language not only gives you additional information about other people and about yourself; it also gives you different information. While people's words tell you only what they consciously want you to know, their body language tells you a whole range of other things, much of which they may not know they're revealing, or even be conscious of themselves. A person's basic personality, the role they're playing, the emotions they feel, the direction of their thoughts, their relationships with others – not to mention what they really think about you – body language communicates it all. And whereas people's words can hide a multitude of secrets, their body language is much more difficult to fake.

Equally, of course, your own body language will – whether you like it or not – transmit information about yourself to others. And studies have shown that what you 'say' non-verbally is often much more influential than what you say verbally, not only because it bypasses the conscious mind of a listener and speaks directly to his or her subconscious, but also because people quite rightly trust non-verbal messages more than they trust words. The bad news is that your body language is making statements about you all the time, and some of these may be things you are trying to hide. The good news is that properly and genuinely used, body language can state what you couldn't possibly say out loud, in a way that really reaches other people: 'I'm competent … I need your support … I like you … I love you'.

Body language isn't only about communication, though. What psychologists have realized over the past decade is that if you change your bodytalk you can actually change all kinds of things about your approach to life. You can, for instance, alter your mood before going to a party, create a better feeling towards your partner, or feel more confident at work. And, of course, if your body language genuinely shifts, and you interact differently with people around you, then they in turn will respond differently to you – so that how you project yourself to others will be reflected back to you, in a neat, circular process.

▼ What's happened? However ambiguous his words, his body language can give his female companion sufficient clues to begin to interpret the call. His serious expression, sympathetically tilted head and ready-for-action stance show he's probably received news that is unexpected, that is worrying but not tragic, and that demands action.

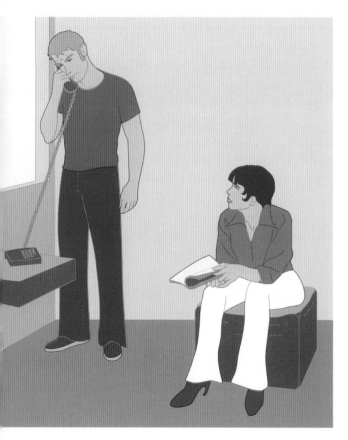

Words of warning

Because body language is such a powerful tool, you need to take care when using it – so, before you begin, a few words of caution!

First, it's a myth that body language allows you to read a person like a book. This theory, which was an attempt to 'alphabetize' non-verbal communication by defining a single gesture as having a single meaning, was originally fashionable in the 1960s. If a person scratched their nose, that meant they were lying. It didn't matter whether the person was scratching because their nose itched, because they were nervous, or because nose-scratching was an important ritual in their sub-culture – they were still seen as lying. Nowadays, we know it's just not that simple. Body language elements differ in meaning, and can only be understood in the context of a person's life situation.

Second, using body language successfully isn't about ignoring the words. Though we humans are apes – and many of the bodytalk sequences we use come directly from those developed by apes – we are nevertheless talking apes. Therefore, much of this book is about using body language along with the words to emphasize them, to elaborate on them, to control them, or even to contradict them. To be a real body language expert, use your non-verbal skills alongside, not instead of, your verbal ones.

Finally, don't think you can use body language to get others to do what you want. People aren't fools. If you try applying non-verbal techniques in order to manipulate someone into liking you, then of course they'll respond to what you do – but they'll also respond far more strongly to those of your actions that reveal your manipulation. They'll register, often unconsciously, your false smile, your shifting eyes, your nervous stutter – and will act accordingly. So if you're expecting to be able to rule the world through body language, you'll be disappointed!

Practise makes perfect

How can you best use body language? The first step is to develop your powers of observation, gathering as much knowledge as possible when you interact with others. Looking is the most obvious way and probably the channel through which you'll gain most information. Listen, too, not so much to people's actual words but to the way those words are said, the way voices sound as people speak. Your other three senses, touch, smell and taste, can also tell you a surprising amount: the warmth and moisture of a colleague's handshake can give you vital clues as to how confident he is about the meeting; a friend's body odour will actually shift if she becomes scared during a horror film; a lover's taste will change as he becomes aroused.

As you become more expert, you'll be able to notice more than just the obvious 'macrocues', such as people's gestures or facial expressions. You'll also be able to notice the much more subtle and even more fascinating 'microcues'.

▲ Bodytalk transforms the meaning of language. If the words that accompany the smiling bodytalk shown here are humorous, then we think nothing of them. If the words refer mockingly to someone else in the room, then the body language takes the edge off the insult. However, if the words referred to something sad or tragic, then the bodytalk totally transforms their impact, making the speakers appear thoughtless and cruel.

So, although at first you only may spot the macrocue of someone's angry clenched fist, in time you'll also register the microcue of their skin colour change when they just start feeling irritated. With practise, your mastery of microcues will let you understand – and even predict – just how those around you are thinking and feeling, and so be one step ahead all the time.

Pay attention to your own body language, too; you yourself are a major source of information. Monitor your external signs, noticing how, as you respond to what's happening, your body position

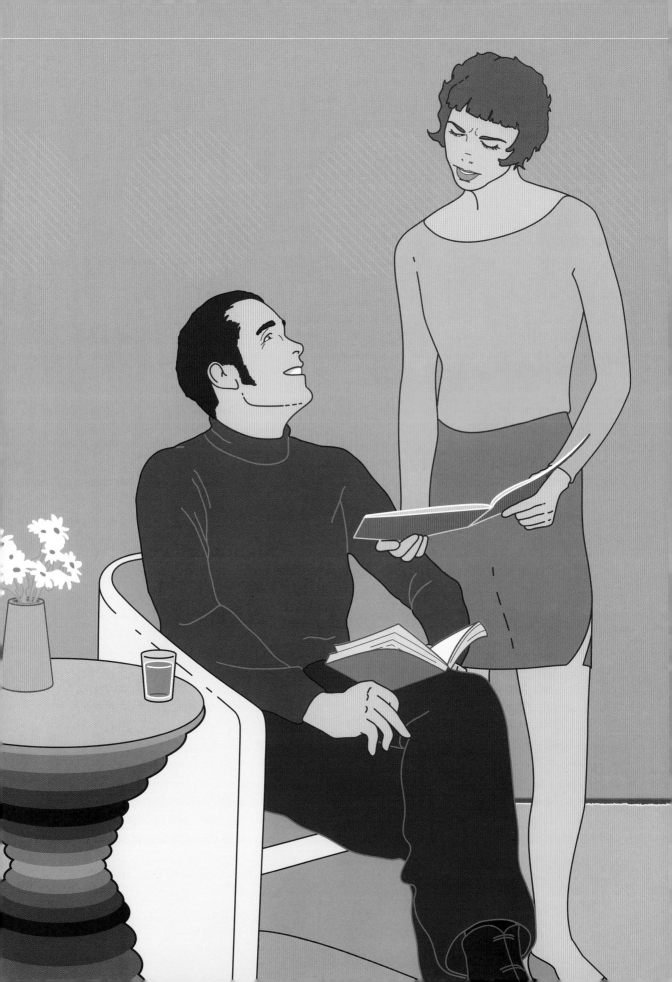

changes, your movements adapt, your voice alters, your breathing shifts. Monitor, too, the internal signals that only you are aware of: the butterflies in your stomach that tell you you're excited, the tension headache that alerts you to stress, the internal picture of your lover's face when you think of him, the internal sound of a friend's voice when you imagine talking to her. These are vital signs of what your body is telling you.

Looking for clues

To know just what to look out for, you need a body language vocabulary. The following are the essential elements of this, the ones on which this book is based.

APPEARANCE Look at a person's height, their natural skin, hair and eye colour, their body shape. Within the limits of cosmetic surgery and the camouflage of clothes, all these things can tell you accurately what a person's gender is, their age, racial background and culture.

STYLE AND IMAGE Notice clothes, hairstyle, make-up, accessories. These usually show you temporary things, such as age, the fashion sub-culture with which a person identifies, their status in society, what kind of job they have, their leisure interests.

◄ **Bodytalk vocabulary helps spell out a situation. This mixed gender couple (appearance) are in a home situation (environment) and standing close enough to touch, so they are probably partners. While her gesture indicates she wants immediate attention, his gesture suggests he's not taking that very seriously. This is confirmed by his relaxed and her tense posture, while their facial expressions hint that he's joking while she's getting irritated. We'd know more if we could hear their voice tone, or pick up their mood from smell, taste and physical functions.**

POSTURE Notice particularly the way someone stands, how they arrange their body, the angle at which they hold their body and head, and the direction in which their arms and legs are pointing. These elements can not only give clues to permanent things, such as upbringing and age, but can also reveal passing thoughts and feelings, especially interest, respect and approval.

GESTURE AND MOVEMENT These are particularly important when used with words, emphasizing and adding emotional 'markers' to speech, rather like the punctuation marks that can give extra meaning to written words. Each person may well also have a personalized set of gestures they regularly use – look especially at torso and limb movements, gestures of hands and feet, and head nods and shakes.

FACIAL EXPRESSION Permanent facial lines built up over time tell us about personality; notice the 'try hard' wrinkles between a person's eyebrows, or the tiny, inward mouth lines that denote a 'withholding' personality. Also important are fleeting facial expressions, such as frowns, that show you how a person thinks, feels and relates minute-to-minute.

EYE MOVEMENT We give and receive more information from the eyes than from any other part of the body. They're particularly vital for showing moods and relationships between people – lovers gaze, competitors stare, while liars often avoid eye contact. Pay attention to gaze direction, eye shape, pupil size, length of gaze and what the eyebrows do.

VOICE Words are not part of body language, but the voice that speaks them is. Voice gives a wealth of information about basic background: culture, class, age, sex, birthplace, colour, race. Some studies even suggest that you can tell a person's

▲ Here appearance, environment and image are the same. But now the woman's posture is relaxed, while his is more tense; her gesture is fluid while his jabbing finger signals irritation; their expressions indicate her humour and his anxiety. The interpretation here is that she is light-heartedly presenting something that, in fact, really concerns him.

height from their voice! Variations in volume, pitch and rhythm also show how we feel and whether something is important to us.

SMELL AND TASTE Everyone has a personal smell and taste 'signature' that builds up in the mouth and in body hair. It can signal a person's general health, food preferences, and feelings of anger, fear, or sexual arousal. Smell and taste are also important in creating a bond between people.

ENVIRONMENT Body language isn't just about what people do, but also about the non-verbal statements they make when they create their environment. Architecture, room size, furniture style, light and temperature preferences, privacy needs, at home and at work, can all tell you what's important to someone, their basic personality, and how they relate to others.

TOUCH Touch, or lack of it, shows how close people are and often indicates that strong emotion is being shared. Touch is also used in conversation to emphasize a point, and in power relationships to show control and dominance.

PHYSICAL FUNCTIONS The body's physical functions, like breathing patterns, heart-rate, blood pressure, skin colour, sweat levels, skin temperature and body fluids, indicate what someone is feeling. They are instant signals both of physical sensation and of emotional reaction.

INTERNAL BODY SIGNS The messages you give from inside are just as much a feature of body language as the ones it manifests on the outside. Be aware of any internal pictures or sounds that you experience when you think of someone or something. Be aware of where any internal sensation is, and what it feels like – moving or still, heavy or light, warm or cold, relaxed or tense.

Decoding the message

Once you've learned to observe closely and accurately, then you can start to work out the meaning of what you're noticing. This isn't as easy as it may seem. As has been mentioned before, one single element of body language may not necessarily have one particular meaning, but several different ones, depending on the specific context and situation.

First, think about a person's background when interpreting what they do. Everyone's body language has its roots in their culture and upbringing; we learn the vast majority of our non-verbal skills when we are children, from the adults around us. Of course there are general signals that everyone uses, so most body language you see will fit the descriptions in this book (though these descriptions are based mostly on Western research and so won't necessarily apply to people from purely African, Asian or Middle Eastern cultures).

Equally, a person's body language will always be personalized. Your best friend's irritated blink may, for example, be your colleague's sign of nervousness. So if you interpret your colleague's body language as meaning the same as that of your friend, you'll spend a great deal of time wondering why she is irritated with you – and trying unnecessarily to calm her down. Watch people's patterns over time to get what non-verbal experts call 'baseline behaviour', which is their normal way of acting.

Also, when you observe a single element of body language, check out thoroughly what else is happening in the situation in which you see it. What can you tell from the person's whole body to gain a complete picture of what is happening? What are their other body signals saying; do they confirm your interpretation or contradict it? How are other people responding to what is happening; do they see things differently from the way you do? What occurred just before and just after what you have seen that will help to put it in context and give it more meaning?

You should also look out for short set sequences of body language signals that always occur together; for instance, when someone is startled by an unexpected noise, laughs to release the tension, then relaxes with a sigh. By being able to read not only the single cues – the 'words' of body language – but also these sequences – or 'sentences' – you'll be able to understand far more about what is happening.

When such a sequence has developed and become stylized in human social interaction – such as the complex, non-verbal ritual we go through when we say goodbye to someone – it often has a different meaning from a spontaneous sequence; so be prepared to interpret it differently.

You'll also, with practise, be able to spot broad patterns in a person's body language, where several elements combine to tell you something more general than just how they are feeling at this precise moment. Clusters of signals in the way someone stands, looks and talks can show you what kind of person they are or what their attitude to a particular aspect of life is.

Taking action

Once you've observed and interpreted either your own or someone else's body language, then you can act. You can use bodytalk to get more of what you want – to be successful in what you do, to create closer bonds with others, to help or support friends or lovers, to boost your confidence.

When taking action, you have three options. Surprisingly, the first and often the best choice is simply to let your own body language instincts take over, for everyone communicates non-verbally, all the time, as a natural, unconscious part of their lives.

If a close friend is crying and you feel sad for her, then you will automatically lean forward, and your eyes will spontaneously gain a gleam of

▼ This saleswoman falls into a trap typical of bodytalk novices – taking the basics of body language rapport and overplaying them. Her smile is too bright for use with people she's only just met; her forward lean and extended hand intrude on her clients' territory. And she seems oblivious to the fact that they are leaning back, blocking her off with arms and legs, their expressions showing they're not receptive to her words.

moisture that signals your empathy. You don't need consciously to decide to do this; your body will naturally and effectively mirror your feelings. So in many situations, trusting your instincts is the best option.

Your second option in any situation is to talk. As already mentioned, speaking is sometimes the best way to explore a problem, swap experiences, or offer comfort. Remember, though, that when you speak, you'll also be communicating non-verbally. This book will not only help you tell when words are most appropriate, but guide you towards using genuinely effective body language to underline and support those words.

Your final option comes into play when you decide to use some element of body language deliberately, or to deliberately change what you would naturally do. It may be that you feel sympathetic to a friend, but don't know the best non-verbal way to show that. Or it could

be that your natural expressions of sympathy aren't working and you need more options. If so, this book will help by outlining what creates success in non-verbal communication and by suggesting ways you can achieve that success for yourself.

The real work is, of course, up to you. You have to gather information about body language, to start interpreting that information, to practise until you can use body language easily and it has the effect you want. Even if you achieve all this, bodytalk may not offer the answer to all your problems – but it will help you make the most of what you think, what you feel, what you do, and – perhaps most important of all – who you are.

▼ **A more sensitive approach gets better results. A toned-down version of her earlier signals, which respects her clients' space and reflects her relationship with them, means that everyone feels more at ease.**

2 face to face

From the very first moment you interact with another person, your mutual body language is in constant communication. You are telling them about yourself by the way you look, the way you move, the expression on your face and the tone of your voice – and if this sounds just too revealing, then reassure yourself with the fact that they are telling you all about themselves in just the same way.

The body language of interpersonal relationships

This section of the book looks at how the above mentioned process happens through social body language: how you can interpret accurately what others are communicating to you, and how you in turn can be most effective in what you communicate to them. It takes you through the steps from the initial meeting to holding a conversation, from understanding a person minute-to-minute, to analyzing their personality over time. It explores how to make and keep friends, how to defend your time alone and how to respect that of other people, and finally how to survive when you move from one-to-one contact into the world at large.

Nice to meet you

When you first meet someone, you have just 10 seconds to make an impression on them. Or to put it another way, in the first 10 seconds after meeting a new person, you will be making a particular impression on them whether you like it or not. Before you even open your mouth to speak, you non-verbally imprint the other person with your persona – the image you present to the world – coming across as effective or ineffectual, confident or nervous, friendly or stand-offish. Even with someone you've met before, you can determine the whole tone of your contact by what your body language communicates at the very start.

Let's begin, then, with the basics. How do you initially make contact? The most important way humans normally do so is with their eyes, so use yours effectively. Don't use an off-putting stare but do keep your eyes on the person you're about to greet so that, when they turn to you, you're ready to meet their gaze. If you open your eyes just slightly more widely than normal, this approximates the fleeting 'eyebrow flash' that humans give spontaneously when they acknowledge another person, and which will automatically make your companion feel welcomed and appreciated.

After the initial greeting, follow through that eye contact. Humans naturally turn towards those that they respect and value, so let your body and head direction focus on the other person and fight any temptation to look or move away, as it signals, 'I'm nervous…', 'I feel inferior to you …'. You'll be much more impressive if you face directly, lean in slightly, and display confidence and friendliness with a smile. (A good trick to remember if you're nervous and finding the encounter difficult is to smile quickly and widely three or four times, rather than try to maintain a fixed grin, which will die away slowly and embarrassingly.)

Then you will be ready to move into a formal greetings ritual involving words and touch. The direction in which your body is turned and angled towards the other person can automatically extend itself into offering your hand to be shaken. Don't fight shy of this; humans are programmed to feel closer to someone they've touched, so missing out that part of the ritual means you lose the chance to create a bond.

A useful tip to remember from politicians, incidentally, is to forget worrying about what to say, and simply repeat the person's name as you look and touch. This not only makes your companion feel important, but links the person's name and face in your mind, making recall easier at a later time.

Throughout, of course, you won't be acting in a vacuum. The other person will be giving you clear signals as to whether they approve of what you're doing. Keep checking constantly to see how friendly or formal they want to be, and then adapt those five separate elements of your greeting: eye contact, body lean, smile, touch and words. If meeting an opponent in a crucial sports match, for example, you may want to tone down the smile and shake hands crisply and briefly. But if your sister's new fiancé seems to think he should kiss you on both cheeks and you want to make him feel at ease, move closer in response to his extended forward lean, and gauge from his movement just the right time to offer first one cheek, then the other.

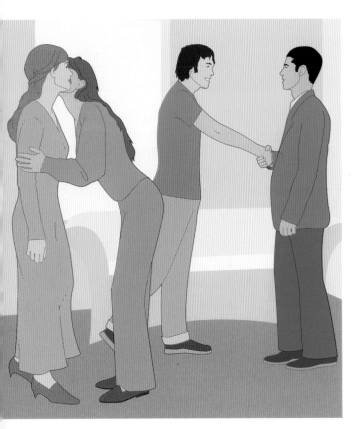

◀ As one couple visits another, a male handshake indicates formal respect (and originally showed good intentions by offering a hand free of a weapon). Direct body-facing, eye contact and a smile show friendship, but in Western society, at any rate, male friends often keep their arms at full stretch to maintain space between their bodies as they greet. Women on the other hand, are more likely to opt for body contact, with hands touching arms and a 'social' kiss on the cheek or in the air. Notice though how both women are slightly wary, one keeping her hands by her sides and failing to reach out, the other seeming to lean forward but in fact pulling back sharply from the waist. Why are they acting in such a way?

▶ In this subsequent illustration, we may have the answer. While the couple in the background show the hand-to-arm greeting typical of a man and woman who aren't partners, the foreground couple don't. Their full-body contact and her delighted smile suggest that maybe they are more than just friends! No wonder there is tension in the air.

Creating rapport

However long you've known a person and whatever the context of your relationship, there'll be a short phase of 'settling in' after the initial greetings are over. Outwardly, you may seem just to be exchanging basic information about yourselves; in fact, there will be a lot more going on on a non-verbal level as you align your individual body language styles in order to adjust to that complementary body language rhythm called 'rapport'.

Achieving rapport is an instinctive human skill. Babies do it even before birth, when their heartbeats and body functions have a rhythm that matches those of their mother. By a few months old, they will already have learned the other main element of rapport, 'turn-taking' – baby gurgles and smiles, mum responds with a coo and a grin, baby gurgles and smiles again.

As adults, we no longer resort to gurgling to get a response! We do, however, use non-verbal cues to both 'match' and 'turn-take'. You match when both of you take up the same body posture, unconsciously copy gestures, or emphatically nod just when your companion is emphatically saying a particular phrase. You turn-take instinctively, alternating remarks, movements and smiles. When your rapport is really good, the words aren't important – your complementary body language says it all.

But what if things aren't going well? People's bodies move to very different rhythms and there can be a mismatch. The symptoms are obvious and uncomfortable. You feel ill at ease without knowing why. One of you gets itchy to speak, while the other won't hand over the chance to talk. Instead of seamless turn taking, you butt in and trip over each other – or the silences get longer.

At this point, you may think it's because you have nothing in common. Your discomfort, however, is much more likely to be due to a mismatch not of interests but of body language (especially if your acquaintance is new and you haven't yet learned whether you're compatible). Quite simply, your rhythms don't fit.

If you want to take action to feel more comfortable with another person, use this body language technique: quite simply, match their rhythms actively instead of leaving it to chance. Observe the other person's posture, then move easily into copying it. If they change posture, do so too. Notice their rhythm of words and gestures, and follow it – a tiny nod when they nod, a slight lean forward when they say something emphatically, a flicker of a finger to mark their gestural rhythm. Be so tuned in to your companion that you turn-take naturally, speaking when they stop, slowing down when they want to start.

For the first few minutes, deliberately matching an alien rhythm will feel uncomfortable; if it didn't, your body would already have done it automatically. And you have to be subtle about what you're doing or the other person may feel mocked or mimicked. The secret is to keep your movements small and your paralleling shifts of posture or expression barely noticeable.

Keep going, though, and two things will eventually start to happen. First, with practise, your body will feel more at ease and comfortable. Second, as the other person is reassured by the way you are synchronizing your responses with theirs, they will begin to synchronize themselves more with you, following your natural rhythm, moving into your natural position, smiling when you smile. Your two rhythms will coincide; you will be in rapport.

▸ **They're each interested in what the other is saying, but there are still some reservations. Check their direct eye contact, friendly expressions and direct-facing posture – as set against the distance apart they are standing and her slightly nervous hand gesture.**

▲ Rapport fades. He's trying to impress – but, in fact, his direct gaze, pointing finger and arm sweep are aggressively intrusive. Her arms are up to protect herself and she's averted her gaze and blanked out her expression to signal her withdrawal.

▲ Rapport builds again. The distance between them has closed, their movements are more animated, and their smiles are wider and more genuine. Even his hands-on-hips gesture, which in some contexts could seem threatening, is part of the fun.

The art of conversation

It may be a cliché, but it is nevertheless true that the key to successful conversation is good listening – this is what makes other people enjoy talking to you. But good listening isn't only about asking relevant questions.

The constant non-verbal signals of your interest are actually more vital than your occasional verbal queries, however well phrased.

The best way to send the right signals is, of course, genuinely to listen, blocking out your own thoughts and focusing on what your companion is telling you. If you do this, you'll spontaneously offer the body language that a good listener does: you'll look at your companion, you'll naturally lean towards them and angle your head slightly to one side in order to hear them better. You won't fidget or fiddle; your body will remain still and attentive, except for any slight matching of posture or gesture.

For extra impact, you can also 'raise the volume' on your body language signs of attentiveness. Humans are biologically programmed to feel good when they get a reaction from someone else, so the more feedback you give to someone who is talking, the more appreciated they'll feel.

Begin by angling your body towards the person who's talking and you will be offering a non-verbal invitation to speak.

Follow up by the regular head nod, which in human beings shows understanding. Make sure you nod clearly and in synchrony with what your companion is saying, showing your comprehension just when they're emphasizing an important word or phrase. If they make a really important point, give a long, slow nod, which says, 'I'm taking you seriously'. Be wary, though, of the 'nodding dog syndrome'; irrelevant nods signal that your mind is wandering, double nods tell others to speed up their rate of talking, while triple nods may bring people to a confused standstill.

Also take care to reflect your companion's emotions. When someone speaks, what they want is for others to laugh or cry along with them. So if your companion laughs, make sure you at least smile; if their bodytalk shows sadness, let your expression become serious; if they get angry as they recount a story, mirror that irritation by making your head nods faster and sharper.

And if you ask a question, add a slight tilt of the head, frown or half-smile. This says, 'I want to know more, not because you've been unclear, but because you've been so fascinating'. This sign helps you query what someone is saying without threatening them, to encourage them to explain further. There is only one drawback – your companion may believe you're so fascinated that they carry on talking for hours!

THE GOOD TALKER Ever listened to a computerized voice, stripped of all visual and tonal signals, and become confused and irritated? If so, you'll know that it's body language that gives speech meaning, adding vital extra information about what's being said, creating mood and giving emphasis.

The first rule when speaking is to keep non-verbal contact with your listener. This contact can get forgotten as you concentrate only on the words. For example, it's natural to look away regularly when you speak, to help the thinking process (see page 45); so it can be tempting to lose eye contact completely. If you catch yourself doing this, deliberately glance at your listener whenever you can, to include and involve them.

In addition, make sure that your bodytalk reflects what you're actually saying. The most interesting speakers tend to use gesture, voice tone and facial expression in order to clarify and highlight their speech. So be aware of the words and phrases you use that are important to you so that you can give them the necessary emphasis. There are points of emphasis in every sentence, from 'Can you get me a new shampoo?'

▲ She's listening with interest to what's being said – her forward lean, head tilt, smile and wide eyes show how much she's enjoying the conversation.

through to 'Not that way, this way!'; non-verbally stress these points in particular.

Instinctive ways of doing this include: raising or lowering your tone, slowing down your speech, widening your eyes, beating out the emphasis with a nod of your head or a wave of your hand (known as a 'baton gesture' because it looks as if you're conducting your own personal verbal orchestra). Of course, if you're not used to varying your body language like this to create interest, you may initially overdo it, and feel silly or embarrassed. So first watch how others succeed, then experiment gradually with gestures or voice tones that come naturally.

To achieve this, note the words that are important to you, the ones you automatically stress; then exaggerate that vocal stress a little, with tone, pitch or speed. Add in movement – a head nod, then a minute forward lean that takes the head nod one stage further. Use the baton gesture, letting your 'leading' hand (usually the right one) mark your head nod with the kind of

▲ Her right-hand baton gesture rhythmically emphasizes a point she's making, while her slight body tilt adds further weight to important words.

▲ A handover gesture to the listener – marked by an outstretched open palm, as opposed to the down-directed hand and pointing finger of her baton gesture. Her less animated expression here shows that she's no longer expecting attention, but is ready to listen.

movement that is most spontaneous for you. One good way to rehearse all this is on the phone; that way, there'll be no startled glances when you wave your arms about!

Finally, show genuine feeling in your speech. Be aware of anything you say that has an emotional undercurrent. Allow yourself to experience some of that emotion: the embarrassment you felt when you dropped the spaghetti, the shock you felt when the waiter spilled the soup. Then let your body show your emotion naturally (see page 69);

allow your voice to reflect it slightly in tone and pitch, and your face to mirror it subtly in expression, particularly through your eyes, eyebrows and mouth, the primary channels for emotional communication. You'll draw your listener into your experience, making it far more vivid for them.

BALANCING ACT Much of the art of conversation lies in creating a balance between everyone's contribution – an extension of the turn-taking rhythm of rapport described earlier. Successful speakers control this balance by using non-verbal signals to show they've finished speaking, or that they want to contribute. Unfortunately, not everyone knows these signals, uses them or responds to them.

If you're the listener, it's useful to know that when a speaker pauses for longer than usual or slows down their speech, they're probably ready for you to talk. They may accompany this with a shift in voice pitch, direct eye contact and a small 'hand-over gesture' that waves you in to take your turn. The secret, for you as listener, is not even to attempt to talk unless you see these things happening, or you'll find yourself interrupting. If, when the signals do occur, you actually don't want to contribute, then as well as the verbal trick of asking another question to urge the speaker on, you can decline your turn by keeping eye contact and nodding slowly, or by using the 'query expression' mentioned on page 25.

If you are the speaker, make the above signals obvious when you want to hand over. Equally, don't give such signals if you want to keep talking. (If someone interrupts you, it's often not because they're rude, but because you've given some ambiguous non-verbal sign in the middle of a sentence.) If you want to hang on to your turn, avoid eye contact, don't pause, raise your voice slightly and prevent yourself making any turn-giving gestures.

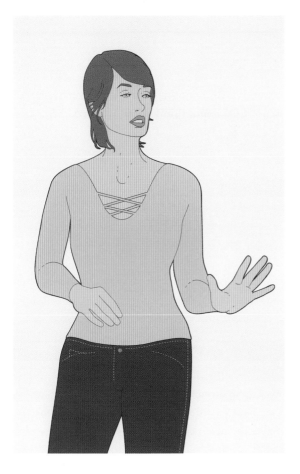

▲ She wants to interrupt. Her slightly uptilted hand and head hint at a 'stop' gesture, and her slightly open mouth means she's probably just breathed in, ready to talk; the sound of that breath is another non-verbal cue to the speaker that she wants her turn

The worst conversational problem is not getting to take a turn at all. If you're stuck with the party bore mentioned earlier, begin by giving him (or her) the natural signals we make in conversation when we want to speak. Get eye contact and at the slightest pause, breathe in audibly as if you're preparing to say something and give a short cough to bring the attention to you. Increase your rate of nodding to give the message 'Hurry up and finish'.

If all this fails, be anti-social. Hard-heartedly stop giving the normal good-listener signs. Lose eye contact, stop nodding, blank your expression to give no emotional feedback. Look to one side as if distracted. Raise a finger or hand – a sign we learn in school that still, for adults, means, 'I want to talk'. If, after all that, your companion still continues, he isn't worth listening to; interrupt mercilessly until he gives you attention, and use that opportunity to move on.

It goes without saying that if you yourself receive any of these 'I'm bored' body language signals when you're talking, there's only one correct response – a courteous and immediatè hand-over, and an inner resolution to shut up and listen for a while.

Mind magic

Whenever you interact with someone, you naturally learn more about them and the way they think. Recent body language discoveries suggest that with a keen eye and ear, you can understand what people are thinking and how their minds work in very specific ways. According to psychologists, our body language gives clues to how our brains are working. Quite simply, what we think about inside our heads, we express externally with our bodies.

As you probably know from your own experience, the people and experiences that we encounter in the outer world around us all have some inner association in our heads – perhaps in the form of a picture, a sound, or even a smell, taste or touch. (If you doubt that you do this, remember what colour the sheets are on your bed at the moment, or imagine what your favourite track would sound like played at half speed.) Everything we store in our brains has a representation there – even if we aren't able to see a totally vivid picture of it or hear a completely clear sound.

So, to interpret the body language clues to what is going on is someone's head, begin with the simplest deduction: how is a person using their thought processes? Two American psychologists, Richard Bandler and John Grinder, have suggested that a person's eye movements show which sense they're thinking about – in other words, whether they're remembering or imagining something seen, heard, touched, smelled or tasted.

Bandler and Grinder suggest that if what a person is thinking about is something they have seen, they'll look up or defocus, sit up, raise their eyebrows, furrow their brow horizontally and breathe more quickly. If they're thinking about a sound, they'll look to the side, tilt their heads as if listening and breathe evenly. If what a person is thinking about is a feeling (a sensation or an emotion) they'll look down and to the right, lean forward, round their shoulders, breathe deeply.

More specifically, if a person is remembering something that they actually saw or heard, their eyes will also slightly move to their left – but if they're imagining seeing or hearing something that hasn't actually happened yet, their eyes will move to their right. If they're thinking in words (what you might call 'talking to themselves') then they'll look down and to their left, and often make tiny movements of throat or lips.

Each of these eye movements takes less than a fraction of a second; you may not even register them. They'll be strung together in sequences of several dozen, and so you can't possibly track

▲ Eye and head movement show that her thoughts are on something she has seen – and that she now 'sees' that picture in her mind's eye.

▲ The slight tilt of her head and her eye position show that she's recalling something she's heard.

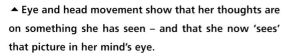

▲ Her 'down and to her left' gaze shows that she's talking to herself.

▲ A defocused, down-slanted gaze showing that she's remembering a feeling.

every thought as it happens. But you can certainly get a great deal of information about whether someone typically thinks in pictures, words or feelings, and whether any one memory or creative thought is being experienced through any one particular sensory channel. Sometimes, with a clear signal, you can tell whether someone is remembering what they've seen, and ask, 'What did they look like?', before they have told you their thought.

MIND MOVEMENTS Having got a broad idea of what someone is thinking of through their eye movements, you can then start being more specific by also watching their head and limbs perform what are known as 'mime movements'. Try asking someone how many glasses of wine they had last night. They will 'see' in their mind's eye by looking slightly upwards; their eyes may also 'fix', from left to right, with a tiny stare to mark each item they're remembering. The rest of

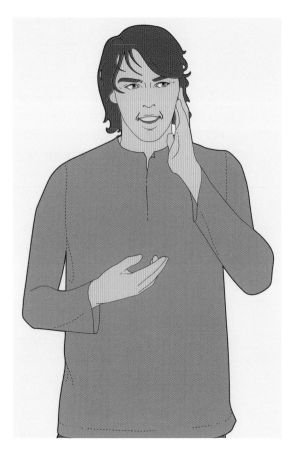

▲ Luke talks about a minor bike accident he actually had recently. His hand gesture shows just where he hurt himself, and his wide eyes and mouth recall his surprise. But his expression also shows that now he feels quite sanguine about it – he's almost enjoying recounting the tale. We often show graphically, through using our hands, how an event has affected

us; particularly if we've had a strong sensation in a particular body part, we'll draw attention to that part with our gestures.

▲ Romily talks about something that she is actually planning to do in a few weeks' time; she 'sees' the future off to her right (and the past off to her left).

their body will add extra information: their head may give a tiny nod for each fix; they may tap out, with a finger, hand or foot, the exact number that they recall. With careful observation and precise interpretation, you will not only be able to tell what they were going to say, but also, if what they say doesn't fit with what you saw, you can challenge the inaccuracy.

Head and limb movements, in particular, give a remarkable amount of information about how we 'see' things in our heads. So, for example, the shape a person traces with their hands and head will be representative of a shape they're visualizing in their minds. The relative size of what they draw will tell you the relative importance of things to them. The speed at which they make movements will show how you how much excitement, tension or satisfaction they feel about what's in their mind. The position of their gestures in the air may well indicate whether what they're thinking about happened in the past (gesture to the left or behind), present (gesture directly in front) or future (gesture to the right or far in front). And if their movement equates a real action, that may well indicate that they've done that action or are intending to do it.

Try this test: without explaining why, ask a friend to describe her job. Watch the movements she uses. She may trace several stabbing movements with her hands while at the same time she shakes her head sharply from side to side. Her movements may start high in the air when she talks about her boss and gradually descend as she refers to her colleagues. Her gestures may speed up as she goes into detail about just what her latest project involves, moving from the left as she describes starting it until eventually, as she imagines finishing it, she makes a large, chopping movement over to her right. Even with no words at all, you'll be able to guess at her real compatibility with her job – just as you would if she gave a completely different picture by using gentle, flowing gestures to trace a circle in the air before finally lifting her hands in a harmonious and relaxed way.

Emotional expressions

Finally, as you watch eye movements and check gestures, observe a person's facial expression, for that will show you just how they feel about what they're saying. The sequences are straightforward to read, though they can be minute, fleeting and extremely variable. Some of the more common expressions are: a slight smile and a widening of the eyes as if to 'see more', showing a person feels good; a slight frown, a down-drooping of the mouth and a narrowing of the eyes to 'see less', indicating disapproval; a sideways movement of the mouth and a screwing-up of the eyes, showing that they're wary or unsure.

With practise, particularly with someone you know well, you can become remarkably accurate at 'mind reading'. So if, when asked which club she went to last night, your friend first looks up and to the left, then sideways and left, then down, she's probably imagining what the club looked like, what the music was like, and what sensations she experienced. Put all that together with her blank expression when she looked up; a curl of the lip, a headshake and a pushing-away gesture when she looked to the side; and a slight smile and self-touching movement when she looked down. If you know your friend sufficiently well to put meaningful flesh on the bones of her non-verbal communication, you might be not too far off the mark when you guessed that the decor was neutral, the music was awful – but there was someone there she felt good about.

Reading personalities

Using body language to analyze someone's personality isn't something new. As far back as the Middle Ages, people thought that physical appearance had a one-to-one correlation with character. A big nose in a man, for example, meant that he had a large sexual appetite, for reasons that are fairly obvious; a small head meant that someone was unintelligent. This medieval body language was fairly soon discredited – our body 'parts' simply don't indicate what we are like as people.

More recently, psychologists have been re-thinking this. For while the elements we inherit, such as a large nose or a small head, bear no relation to what sort of person we are inside, the elements of our body language that we build up over the course of a lifetime do. If, for example, someone is an easy-going person and very relaxed, her body posture will be loose and fluid because this is how her muscles are. Conversely, if she is very nervous and tightens her muscles a great deal of the time, then she may end up with tense, raised shoulders.

If you want to gauge someone's character, don't look at their individual gestures or fleeting expressions. Look instead at their more perm-anent, consistent, life-long body language patterns – typical posture, common gestures, usual sequences of eye movement, expression and touch. With this checklist in mind, observe a person over time and you'll be able to draw conclusions about what their patterns mean.

To start you off, this section covers three commonly recognized personality structures, and goes on to describe the body language that often goes with them.

LOOKER, LISTENER OR TOUCHER? One element underlying everyone's personality is which of the senses they favour. Does someone revel most in what they see, hear or touch? (The senses of smell and taste are usually peripheral, important only in situations such as eating or love-making.) Most humans do have a slight preference for one of these, but some people have an extremely distinct liking for one sense or the other, which informs their personality and can frequently show through visibly in their body language.

Lookers tend to have good posture but tense shoulders. They're often thin with tight lips. Obviously they'll choose clothes and furniture for visual impact – they feel good inside when they see attractive things. Not only this, but they also think mainly in pictures, which causes horizontal brow furrowing (see page 121), so they may have forehead wrinkles on an otherwise unlined face.

Listeners think sound is important – words as well as noises. Their usual posture is with head slightly down and to one side, as if listening, or with one hand up to their face or ear – the 'telephone posture'. When thinking something through, you'll often see their lips move, as if talking to themselves. They love rhythm, and may beat out mental riffs on tables, chair arms or in the air. They'll have the car stereo set to switch on when they turn the ignition key

Touchers – who are typically very emotional people – are often rounded in shape. They may not actually be plump, but they tend to lean in, have slightly rounded shoulders, and full lips. They breathe deeply, move in a rather loose, relaxed manner, and often have deep voices. Their style is based on how things feel rather than look, so they will choose for comfort and softness rather than fashion.

There are pros and cons to each sensory preference. Having a leaning towards one rather than another does not put a person at a disadvantage in life, though it may mean that they are more suited to some tasks than others. Never, for example, ask a listener to tell you what to wear to a party, while fashion advice from a looker will ensure that you look superb – but won't guarantee you feel comfortable. Equally, if you notice that your interior decorator is a toucher, you may want to hire someone else – though you might also consider having a sensuous affair with him!

Check to see if you yourself have a strong preference for one sense. If you have, prepare for potential problems when you meet someone with a strong preference for another. If you're a looker and your friend is a listener, drawing him a picture of your new flat will be useless; tell him about it instead. If he, in return, tries to describe his new girlfriend, you may need him to show you a picture before you can really be enthusiastic about the relationship.

Even more subtly, lookers, listeners and touchers differ in their basic communication styles. A looker will, literally, need to look a lot while talking – which may make a listener feel invaded; meanwhile, a listener, who tends to look away while speaking, may make a looker feel unappreciated. And if, during a row, your toucher friend moves closer to get reassurance, he isn't invading your space, just following his sensory preference; if you hug him, he'll find it easier to feel good again.

INTROVERT OR EXTROVERT? Another well-established personality distinction is that between extrovert and introvert – people who consistently like to be sociable as compared with people who

▲ In any social situation it's pretty clear who are the extroverts and who are the introverts. The women are at ease, smiling, holding eye contact, and leaning towards each other. His focus, however, is internal, distancing himself by his position, his lack of eye contact, and his slumped posture. He's very ill at ease with the intense interaction on his right – so he's withdrawn into himself.

prefer a quieter life. Physiologists now believe that there is an actual physical difference between the nervous systems of these two personality types. Introverts are more easily stimulated by interaction and so reach saturation point more quickly; extroverts are less easily stimulated and need more personal contact to feel satisfied.

Introverts' non-verbal patterns will usually protect them from stimulation. They often have an upright posture, a 'stiff-necked' stance or raised-shoulder posture that literally makes it difficult for them to turn to someone else. They will keep their distance, usually backing off if someone moves close. Needless to say, they won't initiate touch themselves, and they may also stiffen in defence if you brush against them. They commonly don't use much eye contact or, if they have to, they'll make 'escape movements' with their feet or hands, as if trying to get away.

Not surprisingly, extroverts act very differently. They will spontaneously turn towards people, lean forward and keep eye contact for long periods of time. They talk more energetically than introverts do, to encourage other people's responses and the stimulation that gives them. Their gestures and expressions seem more cheerful when they're with you simply because they feel excited and comfortable when around others. They touch more, and respond to touch, perhaps by snuggling up in an attempt to get yet more sensation.

Each personality type should be treated differently. Draw an introvert off into a quieter area, or one where you can be alone. Don't invade her space, either by moving closer or by demanding too much eye contact; talk quietly and use touch with care. Bear in mind that it's not that she doesn't like you – it's that your presence may be too much for her to deal with. An extrovert, conversely, can take all the stimulation you can give. Move closer, talk faster, give eye contact, and touch her.

Be prepared, too, for extremely different relationships with each personality type. You alone may not be enough for the extrovert, who will usually like to be out and about socializing with others in noisy, stimulating environments. The introvert will be at her happiest in intimate situations, with dim lights, soft music, and one-to-one contact.

OK AND NOT OK A third personality distinction is that between the 'OK' person and the 'Not OK' person. Eric Berne, the founder of the psychological school of Transactional Analysis (TA), which defines our approach to life in terms of the roles we use in our transactions with others, coined these terms to describe two basic personality types – the person who is basically content with themselves, and the person who feels inferior and insecure.

An OK person's basic posture is upright, with shoulders firm and square, head raised and her body evenly and easily balanced. She moves briskly and without hesitation, and her expression is lively, with a permanent half-smile. If you get close to her, you may notice minuscule lines at the corners of her mouth that slope upwards – a sign that she smiles more than she sulks.

A Not OK person's posture is fractionally hunched, her back slightly bent; she may look slumped as she walks or sits, with head down towards her chest. Her movements are slow, weary and forced, and her expression tired and sad. Her mouth corner lines slope slightly downwards, which is a sign that she sulks more than she smiles.

If you meet a Not OK person you'll be automatically wary. You may feel, without knowing why, that although they are quite lively at this particular party, in the long-term they won't be much fun to be with. Such feelings are instinctive and should be heeded. Humans have an inbuilt defence mechanism that – unless overruled by duty or compassion towards another person – alerts them to the non-verbal signs of someone who suffers long-term unhappiness, and cautions them to steer clear.

People with Not OK body language are at a social disadvantage, finding it difficult to make contact and maintain relationships. And, because body language becomes more fixed with time, such people may find themselves becoming more and more isolated. Be warned! Look in the mirror and be honest with yourself – what does your body language say about you? Is it sliding towards the OK or the Not OK?

If you are the latter, take steps now. For an immediate effect, try adopting the OK body language that you lack. Sit more upright, move more quickly, smile more, and take 'upwards' as your body language direction. This will not only signal more positive things to other people, but will also actually make you temporarily feel better about yourself. The maxim 'Put on a happy face' actually does work.

For deeper, longer-term change, though, you'll need to do more than just act differently on the surface. If you really want to alter your personal body language on the outside, you will actually have to shift your attitudes on the inside. If you build your self-esteem through taking charge of your life, then your body language will eventually shift. You'll straighten up, your facial expression will lift, you'll look more cheerful and the change will be genuine and permanent.

▼ As two people brace themselves to discover what news a letter brings, we see non-verbal evidence of personality. Lee shows his essential optimism by his upright posture, open eyes and slight smile – as well as the way he holds the letter high and close to his body, as if expecting the news to be good. Sophie shows her intrinsic pessimism in the tense down-droop of her mouth, the way she bows her head, drops her eyes and holds the letter away from her as if expecting bad news.

Friends together

You're at a party, a conference, or an evening class. You are standing still, looking straight ahead with no expression on your face, clutching your drink. You are acting like this because you're nervous of being rejected if you approach someone, or because you feel that being seen to look for company is a sign of social failure. Although company is what you really want, what you're signalling is just the opposite. Your message is, 'I don't want to be approached. I'm not interested'.

People who are successful in group gatherings are able to combine non-verbal 'activity' with non-verbal 'approachability'. This doesn't mean that they are extroverts (who prefer a great deal of social stimulation, but aren't necessarily socially active in gaining it). Popular people have a strategy of body movement, gesture, expression, and eye focus that keeps them constantly and energetically seeking contact with others.

Begin to practise these tactics the minute you enter a new venue. Walk slowly but purposefully from place to place, 'sweeping the room' to catch people's eyes. Keep moving; you aren't, at this point, going to stop and talk to anyone. Your eye contact is a non-verbal signal to show you're socially available, as well as allowing you to spot other people who feel the same. Keep your expression friendly rather than flirty, with a half-smile and using open gestures. And relax. A confident and approachable person is an attractive figure to others who aren't quite as self-assured.

When you make contact with an individual, make sure it's with someone who, by previously catching your eye, has already signalled their approachability. One of the reasons we may fail socially is that we judge whom to approach by whether they look interesting in general rather than whether they look interested in us in particular. Then we feel rejected when they don't respond positively to a contact that, in reality, they've not invited.

If the person you're approaching is a man, it's best to advance from the side, and if a woman, approach from the front, as these directions are most reassuring to each gender. Research undertaken in 1974 suggests that, as men are traditionally more likely to be challenged face-to-face, and women more likely to be attacked from behind, our bodies instinctively, though momentarily, press the panic button when approached from these directions, even with friendly intent.

The socially accepted ritual is to approach sufficiently close that someone registers your presence. Then stop momentarily for permission to enter their space, which they'll give with continuing eye contact, a reassuring half-smile or an unconscious beckoning gesture. You may give a minute head nod (in apes, this is a gesture of reassurance), and then an answering smile, a move closer and a greeting. You don't need to make excuses for why you've come over. If the person is also on their own, they'll be relieved you've approached them.

If the person you approach is actually accompanied, but their friend has temporarily wandered off to another room, the bar or the toilet, then offer reassuring signals when the friend returns. Your body language needs to say, 'I'm not taking your man ... I'm not annexing your friend ...' You can achieve this by literally making space for the newcomer, noticeably 'opening' the pair you form part of to allow the other person in, turning towards them, making sure that you give them eye contact, and smiling at them for the first few minutes of the interaction. As they begin to feel reassured and start to relax, you'll find that you all naturally shift position to form an equal triangle, settling down to gaining rapport.

▲ Who's the social leader? Eye direction, body lead – and Philippa's foot direction – all indicate that it is Lee (in the white shirt).

▲ When Romily joins, she's almost ignored. She stands quietly on the outskirts and matches body movement as attention turns momentarily to Tim, in the brown shirt.

IN WITH THE IN-CROWD What if you're making contact not with a single person but with more than one? Joining a group can be a real challenge. There is always a period of 'initiation', a time of waiting to be seen as 'OK' before people will really accept you; this has its roots in ape behaviour, where a newcomer has to be thoroughly checked out first in case they are a threat to the colony.

So choose your group with care, judging from the non-verbal signals which one it is best to approach. If loud voices and lots of activity tell you that group members already know each other, they won't easily make you welcome, while groups where one person only is holding forth will make it difficult for you to make your mark. Opt instead for a group that is small enough for everyone to join in, large enough for individuals to turn and talk to each other, or one in which you know someone whom you can use as your passport in.

It's rarely acceptable for anyone to start contributing as soon as they join the group. The exceptions are high-status people such as party hosts or VIPs, extroverts and dominant people who may unthinkingly try to take over when they join a group, and children – who are forgiven as they haven't yet learned the social rules. For everyone else, the unwritten law is that you spend a reasonable time giving non-verbal signals to show you're safe: staying silent, watching whoever is speaking, gradually assuming a rapportful rhythm with everyone else so that you laugh when they laugh and nod when they nod.

You can, though, shorten your 'acceptability' period by exaggerating these signals just slightly so that they are more noticeable and so that people unconsciously see you as safe sooner. So, when you're finally given a chance to speak, follow these guidelines. Usually, you'll get your turn back again quickly, and your position in the group will then be established.

▲ Still matching group posture, Romily makes contact with Lee via gaze and smile. If she can get the attention of the social leader, he will draw others' focus to her.

▲ Romily is 'in'. Lee is 'making way' for her with eye contact and head tilt. The group is also allowing Romily to take the floor, moving nearer and turning to face her.

WHO'S YOUR FRIEND? When you meet a person briefly, your aim is to reassure them; your body language signals safety, approval and rapport. But when you both start to build a friendship, the communication process then shifts from short-term reassurance to longer-term bonding. Non-verbally, your aim becomes to learn as much as you can about each other, to become as similar as you can be.

Here, body language techniques as such are relatively pointless. The process of forming a deep bond with someone is so complex and lengthy that it can only happen on a subconscious level; if you try to hurry the process on with conscious and deliberate actions, your behaviour will appear

▲ The exciting early stages of friendship, shown by a mirroring of posture, smiles – and fashion sense.

false. Where body language comes in useful, though, is in monitoring how the process is progressing, and in building the best environment for friendship.

When you're on track, you'll find that both of you are opening your sensory channels spontaneously – as if to get information from each other – with wider eyes, longer gazes, and 'pricked' ears that can take in more. You'll be giving each other more information, too, by sitting noticeably closer together, facing each other more directly, making your faces more expressive, touching more frequently, and talking more loudly and with greater emphasis.

This isn't the same type of physical closeness you get with a love partner, but you will develop increasingly similar body language sequences that parallel your increasingly similar thoughts and feelings. You can help this process by setting up the right non-verbal environment for development: arranging to go to events together so that you share experiences, and alternating these with more intimate encounters where you can talk deeply with lots of eye contact and physical closeness.

Given these environments, in time, you'll increasingly 'match' (see page 22), either directly matching postures, gestures or movements, or 'mirroring' by copying with the opposite hand or foot. You'll also parallel your friend not so much with the obvious signs of rapport, but by reproducing subtler sequences such as nervous habits and vocal accents.

You may start wearing the same style of clothes, listening to the same type of music, eating at the same kind of restaurant. This isn't just a case of like attracts like. By adopting the same style as each other, you're deliberately telling the world that you're the same sort of person. Anthropologists call these 'tie signs'. They're most obvious in adolescence, where everyone in the same group will go around wearing the same badge or tee-shirt. But adults display tie signs, too – just think of Gucci handbags and health club memberships.

As your friendship develops, you'd expect all this evidence of bonding to grow, which it does for a while. But interestingly, it fades with time as you become increasingly comfortable and familiar with each other. So if you're with a friend you've known for years, maybe since childhood, you often don't give each other obvious attention. You may sit separately, side by side, not touching, not holding eye contact. Your voices are low, almost unstimulated, your postures relaxed and unexcited. You may not obviously match gestures or styles. It can seem as if you're not interested.

What has happened, quite simply, is that the learning phase is over. You know how the other person moves, so you don't need to face them directly to notice it. You sense that you're close, so you don't need blindingly obvious matching or mirroring to prove it. All the evidence of similarity has become very subtly integrated. Your breathing will be in perfect synchrony, your blinks will match to a fraction of a second, and, if one of you turns white with nervousness or pink with embarrassment, the other will pale or colour up slightly, too. When walking along, you won't need to indicate that you want to turn right and cross the road, as you would with an acquaintance. With an old friend, the turn will be made and the road crossed without either of you realizing that microcues took care of everything.

BEING ACCEPTED What if you're aiming to make friends not with an individual but with a group – an existing, established circle of friends. There are more insecurities and hostilities – even if you're introduced as someone's partner, people will worry in case you're a threat. Will you be more attractive or intelligent than existing members? Will you disrupt the group dynamic?

As in any relationship, talking will help. A few extended conversations with individuals will create a bond as you swap experiences and feelings. But don't expect to talk in the group itself for quite some time. Established cliques often effectively gag new members until they are sure of them, by not offering them any turn-taking signs. Trying to defeat this process by butting in or speaking over people can lead to quite a frightening closing of ranks, as you're ignored, 'talked over', or greeted with a polite but stony silence.

Make progress, instead, with your non-verbal behaviour. Be sure that your body language is always unthreatening to individual members and non-challenging to the existing dynamic. Tend not to go first or try to take the lead; hang back for meals, drinks or anything where an informal queue might form. Be aware of unspoken 'territory' laws in the group – don't, for example, sit down before checking whether you have chosen someone's 'special' chair. Note any group customs, such as always watching a particular TV programme, and don't challenge these. Offer to help with low-status jobs like washing-up rather than expecting to do the high-status ones.

▲ Far left, Oliver's 'leader' role is shown by the way most of the group is looking at him – and by the way Andrew is matching his arm position. Lucy, in particular shows by her smile and inclined head that she favours Oliver. Jo is trying to take attention away by making a point with exaggerated hand gestures – but she isn't taking the group with her. Craig, probably a natural introvert, shows by his protective hand gesture that he feels threatened by the group interaction.

The first signs you're being accepted will be non-verbal. You'll be paid more attention in the group, looked and smiled at more, offered turn-taking signals so that you get to speak. When you

do speak, you can then gauge your success by the quality of the silence; is it still polite, with slightly averted inattentive eyes and slight fidgets, or is it relaxed, with head-on-one-side listening and nods of agreement? Notice if you are being offered more closeness and touch, in the form of spontaneous pats and nudges, or an increased willingness to 'squash up' beside you. As time passes, expect to get not only your own literal territory, such as a place at table, but also your own metaphorical territory – for example, a subject where you're regarded as an expert. In the end, body language within the group will develop an empathy of the sort you'd find in a

▲ With Kay's arrival, the dynamic shifts. She's signalling interest to Oliver by her seductive leg position, emphasized by her hand. Lucy's challenging gaze towards Kay shows that she regards her as a threat, and her mouth pout confirms this. Jo has abandoned her effort to get attention from the group and has turned to Craig, who is responding by smiling and relaxing – though his hand position shows he isn't completely at ease yet.

one-to-one friendship, with unconscious matching, a natural awareness of people's moods, and a mutual ability to predict what everyone is going to do next just through body language.

WHEN FRIENDSHIPS END Whether they're one-to-one or group alliances, many friendships fade over time. Furious rows may create unmendable rifts but, more often, people simply lose their common interests and drift apart. You know what you feel about your friends but, given the social convention of not being upfront about such things, how can you tell what they feel about you?

The simple way to check this is to examine all the non-verbal signals. (If you're trying to analyze a group situation, then check the signs between you and each group member.) If you make a slight move towards a friend, they reciprocate – an unwilling friend shies away. If you offer eye contact to an old friend, that's accepted – a retreating friend blinks or can't meet your gaze. A good friend will match you, even if in very subtle ways – a poor friend will mismatch, so that you bump into each other, walk out of step, pass dishes clumsily at the dinner table.

Look, too, at whether your body language still indicates equality. Are you turn-taking in conversation, or is one of you now doing all the talking and the other doing all the listening? Is one of you still expressing emotion, while the other presents a blank face?

Equally, as a friendship dies, you can often spot negative emotions. If a friend fidgets or fiddles, making what are called 'escape movements' with hands or feet during your time together, then you should be wary. If she responds to your need for support with a brisk voice tone, or fails to hide a smile when you are in an embarrassing situation, then the writing is on the wall.

Talking is the best possible way to resolve such problems – a full and frank conversation to settle things one way or another. But what if you feel nervous of speaking openly? What if you're mistaken and a friend is offended – or what if

▶ **The final stages of friendship: postures mismatch, gestures are defensive and eye contact is difficult.**

you're right and she's hostile? In this case, see what happens if you deliberately withdraw from the friendship even more quickly than your friend is doing – non-verbally. Next time you meet, be the one who loses eye contact, mismatches, holds back on emotional expression or sits far away. Let your natural ambivalence show through, indicating by body language that you are unsure of the friendship.

If you keep doing this, one of two things will happen. Either your friend will, with a sigh of relief, think that you too have lost interest and won't contact you again. Or she'll worry and ask you what's wrong. Either way, you'll have moved closer to a decision whether to end your friendship or to renew it again.

Time alone

Up to this point, we have explored only the body language of interaction. In fact, you don't always want company.

Human beings don't need time to themselves only on a daily basis. Fascinatingly enough, we also need it on a second-by-second basis. Although much of our day is spent looking, listening, talking or doing, every three seconds we need to 'slip away', to give our brains time to process what is happening, to think of what we want to say next. The psychological name for this is 'downtime' (as opposed to 'uptime', when we're interacting with the world). Someone in downtime tilts her head away and shifts her shoulders at an angle. She looks to the right or

◀ There are several states of consciousness, marked by body posture, facial expression and eye gaze. Here Sophie is in 'uptime', when attention and mental focus is out to the real world; her animated expression and responsive gaze show she is listening carefully.

left for a fraction of a second, these are known in the trade as 'conjugale lateral eye movements'. She chews her lips, catches her breath. Her mind is in processing mode.

You've certainly already seen people in 'downtime' on thousands of different occasions, but you've probably not known exactly what you were seeing or what that meant. Realizing that someone is in downtime allows you to respond in an appropriate fashion, to keep pace with their thinking and to avoid clashes when, for example, they're trying to remember something in 'downtime', and you're expecting them to interact with you in 'uptime'.

So if someone looks away momentarily when you're talking to them, don't assume they're not interested or attempt to carry on regardless. They're momentarily shut off from the outside world, and you'll get much further if you slow your speech, pause and give them space to think. And if someone slips into downtime when they themselves are talking – typically this will happen at the very start and very end of their contribution – it means they need to think before continuing. Let them. Don't interrupt with a question – and don't confuse downtime signals with hand-over ones (see page 26), and simply launch in with your own comment. Instead, wait until their head lifts and their gaze returns to yours before you interact again.

THE COLD SHOULDER As well as momentary downtime, we all also need extended, solitary downtime. We need it if we're concentrating, if we've been mentally overactive, when we're under strain or to recover from daily stresses.

▲ Here, Sophie is in 'extended downtime', when thoughts and feelings take awareness away from here and now. Sophie's still posture, withdrawn expression and defocused gaze signal to other people that she is thinking, fantasizing – literally in a world of her own.

Don't confuse this need for alone time with introversion, which is a general, deep-rooted sensitivity to stimulation. Those periods when we're desperate for solitude occur in specific contexts when, like sophisticated computers, we need time to process and recover from the mass of stimuli coming in from the outside world.

You probably know when you need alone time. Your body has a clear set of signals to tell you and other people about that need. You'll feel hazy and unstimulated by the outside world. You'll withdraw, move away from others, and avoid eye contact. You may drop your head or raise your shoulders as if to shut off outside stimulation; you'll actually be less likely to hear someone speaking and less able to feel any touch. Your whole body is reducing its ability to receive outside information because it's simply too busy to bother.

▲ Carlye's non-verbal 'go away' signals of hunching her shoulders and dropping her head are being totally ignored by Chas, who is not only entering her personal space (less than 1.2 m/4 ft), but leaning over, staring at her, placing his hands each side of her – literally 'breathing down her neck'.

If you don't get the alone time you need, the internal signals will increase. You'll start to feel nervous, tense and irritated. This is a sign that your body needs help just as surely as if it were hungry or thirsty. So quite consciously and clearly show your body language withdrawal. Bow your head or put your hands on each side of your eyes as 'blinkers' or over your ears as 'plugs'. Close your eyes if you can – the ultimate way of saying, non-verbally, 'Go away. I don't want to be bothered'.

Put up physical barriers, too. Create a wall around yourself with a blocking arm, books, papers, a chair, or that most obvious of buffers, a closed door. Place your own personal 'markers', such as your coat or bag, on each side of you, so people know that they can't sit down or approach. Stick your elbows out and let your whole body caution, 'Give me space'.

You could also utilize the natural 'hostility' signals, which your body uses instinctively to make you appear more aggressive towards people who insist on trying to interact when you don't want them to. You may find yourself frowning, getting tight-lipped or raising your shoulders – the classic 'cold shoulder' treatment. Sending out these signals indiscriminately isn't, of course, a good idea: you may emerge from your hard-won downtime to find you no longer have any friends. But if you really do need to be left in peace for a while, then your body's natural way of protecting you may well do the trick.

▲ A more respectful and effective way of approaching: Chas leans back fractionally so as to seem less threatening, places his hands safely in his pockets – and probably announces his approach verbally so that Carlye is warned well in advance. Even when Carlye turns to face him, the distance between them will be sufficient for her not to feel intruded on.

SORRY TO INTERRUPT What if you're the one on the receiving end of this non-verbal avoidance? First, recognize that such behaviour is not meant personally and that it is a genuine cry for support. The best thing is to steer clear, for doing so will, in the long run, allow you to maintain a better relationship with that person.

If you just have to interact, check or to ask something, someone who needs time alone will respond better if you use a formal 'alert signal' beforehand. So if you're approaching from a distance, halt while still between 4 and 1.2 m (12 to 4 ft) away, within the social distance zone and before you enter the more intimate 'personal' distance zone. Knock on the door, if there is one between you, and clear your throat (a polite signal of interruption used even with mountain gorillas) rather than speaking immediately.

Once you have caught the attention of a person who needs alone time, keep your interaction to a minimum. Cut down on rapport signals. If another person's body is already over stimulated then your close approach, your forward lean, your demand for eye contact will literally result in them undergoing a panic response. Instead, stay back, keep standing to indicate that you're leaving soon, and don't remove any protective barriers. Speak softly, quietly and slowly so as not to overload their system with more stimulation and, as soon as you have what you want, leave.

And be reassured. The human body never takes more alone time than it needs. So in all likelihood, if you respect their needs, the person who's been non-verbally signalling you to go away will very soon start non-verbally indicating that they want you to come back.

Going public

As soon as you step outside your house, you'll notice a shift in the kind of body language people use. Public body language is subtly different from private body language, because you don't know the people involved, and you'll probably never have a chance to get to know them. The result is that, surrounded by all these strangers, your non-verbal communication will often become very defensive in public.

In public, you may well find yourself using a version of 'cold shoulder' body language, acting as if other people aren't actually there. On a crowded train, for example, you may take on a defocused gaze, studiously 'looking through' someone even though their face is only a few inches from yours; you may shrink your neck into your shoulders and mentally 'deafen' yourself to the conversation of the couple next to you – and remain perfectly immobile as if totally unaware that the person next to you has his left arm jammed up against your right ear.

TRAFFIC CONTROL You can't ignore others for ever, though. So a whole set of non-verbal signals has evolved to cope with times when you have no option but to be involved. The most basic kind of interaction is having to move along a street in conjunction with others: you walk in parallel; you overtake and are overtaken; you meet head on. To succeed in these transactions, remember that the worst strategy is strolling, which non-verbally signals to others that you're likely to stop, so makes them frustrated and impatient. Instead, move quickly and purposefully. Give yourself manoeuvring room by 'enlarging' your body, squaring your shoulders and sticking your elbows out. Focus your gaze sufficiently into the middle distance so that anyone approaching thinks you won't see them and instinctively moves out of the way. This strategy will get you along quickly and easily as long as you can keep up the momentum.

If you hit a 'log jam' and get stuck, change tactics immediately and wriggle, making yourself as thin and as small as possible, squeezing past people carefully to avoid body contact. Notice, incidentally, how men in a 'squeeze-past' situation turn towards someone as if to face any possible attack, while women turn away, their arms across breasts and genitals. Remember, too, that human beings have a natural tendency to 'signal' that they want to change direction by pointing their bodies in the direction they wish to go. Signals like this will be registered, often unconsciously, by those behind you, who will then fall back to allow you to make your move.

ARE YOU BEING SERVED? Another common kind of public interaction is with those people who serve you, in stores, restaurants, and hairdressers, for example. The first step to success is to engage. Be clear and forceful; often you're competing with other customers for attention, and often a busy service worker has other things on his or her mind. Shoot your hand up firmly and noticeably as you stand by the side of the road to call a taxi; step forward and look round confidently for eye contact as you enter a restaurant.

Expect some sort of acknowledgement. Look for a smile and head nod, so that you know you've been seen and that action is being taken. If an acknowledgement isn't forthcoming then emphasize your signals rather than simply waiting. Try a wave of the hand or a shift in your posture that catches the person's peripheral vision, or a gesture sufficiently away from your body that it is really noticeable.

The second stage in service interaction is mutual rapport-building. Here, the person who's serving you is working just as hard as you are to gain contact through body language. Don't expect the same kind of 'intimacy' as you get with friends; most service staff are trained not to engage in too much interaction and will feel uncomfortable if you move too close or keep too much eye contact.

Always use clear, non-verbal signals. Because public places are often noisy and words can be misunderstood, and also because you're just 'passing through' and don't have a chance to build up a relationship, you have to show clearly what your needs are. So rather than simply saying which drink you want at the bar, emphasize your choice non-verbally by pointing. And in response to a query, nod or shake your head to highlight the relevant words as well as saying 'yes' or 'no'.

Take particular care in showing when a transaction is complete or incomplete. If you want to indicate to a restaurant waiter that you're ready to order, for example, don't keep the menu open, as this is a signal that you're still deciding. And if you want to ask an extra question of the sales assistant after she's wrapped your goods, use the 'query' gesture of head on one side and slight smile, or the turn-taking gesture of in-drawn breath and raised finger, or she'll automatically move on to the next customer.

Aim to leave service staff with a positive memory of you so that they treat you favourably next time. The best way is to say goodbye using rapportful body language of a smile and direct eye contact to show that you're not 'dehumanizing' them, as many people do. But be aware of the management's attitude; if your body language style makes an employee engage with you too fully, that may mean a reprimand for them later on. Even the friendliest waiter will get edgy if you insist on prolonged attention when he has customers waiting and the boss is watching.

▲ **Body language alone won't protect you completely on the street, but it can help deter attackers. Here Liz looks easy prey, with scared, 'victim' posture, head dropped, shoulders stooped and worried expression.**

WHO'S IN CHARGE? Perhaps one of the most nerve-racking examples of public interaction is dealing with people in authority – a traffic warden strolling by as you're feeding the mete or a ticket inspector coming down the train carriage. For although theoretically they're there to serve you, they're also there to 'police the system'. Their body language is carefully designed to signal superiority; their uniform includes 'height- and width-enhancers' such as a helmet or peaked cap,

▲ Liz's erect posture, head up and direct confident gaze, suggests that she will be well able to cope with whatever may occur. Her arm stretched strongly and protectively over her handbag makes it much more difficult for a bag snatcher to be certain of success.

and their training shows them how to stare you down in a dominant fashion.

Your body language responds instantly and spontaneously to this, whether or not you're guilty of anything. Just watch the reactions of respectable and innocent passengers the next time that ticket inspector appears: necks tilt into a 'heads-down' defensive position; there is a flurry of nervous gestures to find the ticket, and some people will start making 'escape movements' with hands or feet.

So what is the best way of dealing with this kind of situation? Neither 'dominance' body language to stand up to authority nor 'submissive' body language to placate it are the most effective responses: authority figures are trained to be suspicious of both and to react accordingly. Rather, let your body language signal relaxed equality, with just a touch of deference; that will give out the required message of: 'I acknowledge and respect your role here'.

If the police pull you over on the road, for example, allow your body language to signal that you're not a threat. If it's appropriate, remain seated. If the officer asks you to get out of your car, don't pull yourself up to your full height, but keep your shoulders slightly hunched and your head tilted slightly down. Look but don't stare – direct and confrontational eye contact, when combined with other dominance signals, gives a challenging message. And don't immediately move into a full rapport-building sequence, as this can be seen as an attempt to be over-friendly; instead, tone everything down so that you keep a pleasant expression.

Act promptly and helpfully. We're not talking here about snapping to attention; but if required to produce your driving licence, do so willingly and without delay, and if asked questions, answer them in a quiet tone and without hesitation. You may well be feeling shaky, for your body will, as mentioned before, automatically move into 'panic' mode; so try to keep calm, breathing deeply and steadily.

Finally, watch for the moment when the officer mentally 'signs you off'. For there's a point in each interaction when, having given clear signals of dominance to prevent any problems developing, an authority figure relaxes just slightly because they judge you're not a threat. Once this happens, then you can start to respond in a more friendly way to their less controlled gestures, their more relaxed posture, their growing smile. Be aware, though, that if you take this too far, they may feel threatened again; if they move back to their authority bodytalk, you should immediately revert to your previous 'acknowledgement' behaviour.

IN WITH THE CROWD The most involving of public interactions is being in a large crowd. This might be because the crowd is happy and you're emotionally stimulated by what's happening. It might be because the crowd surrounds you and you're physically stimulated by what's happening. Whichever it is, your body language will be affected not only externally but also internally, and you may react in a number of different ways.

If being with a lot of people excites (as it does many people who have extrovert elements), you may feel good inside. At a concert or sporting event, you may have bursts of adrenaline in your stomach or feel light-headed. This is not only because the added input is stimulating all your senses but also because, when a lot of people get together, they begin to match each other on a very deep level. There is something peculiarly satisfying about being in an audience or even a congregation where everyone jumps to their feet at the same time to applaud.

But if instead of getting excited you become overwhelmed, then you can start to feel bad. Your body will signal panic. You may feel sick and trembly, angry and aggressive. You may at first lose energy and behave in a way that's more passive and compliant; we instinctively do this so as not to challenge the crowd. But if you still feel bad, then you'll start to move in an uncoordinated fashion, changing colour or breathing heavily as your body signals that it's under threat.

Alternatively, you may find yourself joining in the rhythm and deeply matching other people's body language and, because of this, doing all kinds of things you wouldn't normally do. If you start to suffer any of the negative symptoms just mentioned, act immediately. Remove yourself from the situation, even if only for a little while; get away from the movement and the noise. If you can't, stop shouting and moving with the crowd and simply stay still; hide your eyes and block your ears until things calm down.

3 love signs

Whether you've just found romance
or you are trying to make
an existing relationship
work, words are often
totally unimportant – it
is what you do rather
than what you say that counts.

The body language of sexual relationships

This section of the book explores the subtle ways in which your non-verbal messages may make or break relationships. It describes the body language signs that can first bring you and a partner together, how to signal interest and pair up, and then how to develop your relationship sexually. It also looks at body language signs of emotion, outlines some of the ways that body language can help you identify and solve problems, and shows you how to cope with the bad times. Finally, this chapter looks at the non-verbal signals of love, in all its stages.

Love at first sight

So how does a person need to look in order to find love? It's a myth that physical attractiveness is the key to finding love; it's not. Attractive men and women are, it is true, more likely to receive attention; recent research suggests that eye contact with a beautiful or handsome person actually stimulates a specific pleasure centre in the brain. But people are drawn to personality as well as to looks, so physical attractiveness is only one of the elements involved in partner choice. In addition, research has shown that most people are wary of someone who is considerably more attractive than they are and are likely to choose a long-term relationship with someone of equal attractiveness.

So what can be said about what appeals? Despite accusations that men are more interested in a woman's body than in anything else about her, research shows that both genders are initially attracted by a prospective partner's face. This makes sense: the face shows both essential personality and transitory mood. What attracts about it is normality. Recent studies into attractiveness have shown that the more a face approximates the mathematical norm in a particular society, the more appealing it will be to other people. This tendency to prefer the conventional is innate, with babies as young as two months old responding more positively to 'normal' faces than to unusual ones.

Above and beyond this instinctive trend, there is evidence that most women prefer men's faces to look more 'adult', while men prefer women's faces to look younger and more 'childlike'.

Whether or not we like this implication about men and women's respective roles, a man with a strong jaw, chin and nose who gives off signals of being mature, effective and able to protect may well seem more attractive to the opposite sex. Conversely, a woman who shows 'infantile' signals – baby signs such as a small nose, high cheekbones and clear skin, which trigger in all humans a nurturing instinct – will appeal to a man's protective instincts, a fact that may explain why smooth skin and bobbed noses are often the aim of women who have beauty treatments and cosmetic surgery. Interestingly, though, as women move more into dominant positions in society, 'adult' elements, such as a large nose or firm chin, are increasingly seen as feminine and attractive.

When it comes to the key facial feature, the eyes, then in general the larger and paler the better – because of a basic human reflex. When we are interested in something, the pupils of our eyes automatically dilate. The message this sends to the person we're gazing at is that we find them attractive; they feel flattered, and in turn find us appealing. Large, pale eyes show dilation more obviously, so they look both more attracted, and hence more attractive, to the opposite sex.

Colouring has an influence, too. Many people are aroused by those with skins differently coloured from their own, although the majority form lasting partnerships with those from a similar racial background. As for hair colour, the theory that blondes have more fun seems to be true; surveys show that, in Western cultures at least, blonde women (including 'out-of-the-bottle' blondes) are thought by men to be more extrovert and bubbly – though also less intelligent and less dependable as long-term partners. Brunettes are thought to be more serious, intelligent and powerful, while redheads are seen as passionate and moody.

Body appeal

What attracts about a partner's body? Both men and women appear more intelligent and powerful if they're of medium height or above – that is, between 1.6 and 1.7 m (5 ft 4 in and 5 ft 8 in) for a woman, and 1.7 and 1.8 m (5 ft 8 in and 6 ft) for a man. A much taller woman can appear intimidating; it's still true, even today, that all but the most confident of men like to have their own physical stature emphasized by contrast. Being smaller than about 1.7 m (5 ft 8 in) can be a romantic advantage for a woman, though; as mentioned before, many men feel drawn to and protective of women who look small and vulnerable.

A man who is taller than average won't suffer the same problems as a woman will, and in fact is more likely to succeed both romantically and professionally, because the non-verbal image he conveys is that of being confident and effective. A small man, however, can be at a distinct disadvantage because his height gives the opposite impression. Studies have shown that small men who do succeed in life or love can, however, actually be much more effective than their averagely sized counterparts – they tend to develop stronger personalities and increased social competence in order to compensate for an unprepossessing appearance.

When it comes to shape, men do assess a woman on her figure, though less so than on her face, and the less so the older the man. As far as specific body parts are concerned, legs, bottoms and breasts seem to be the areas that men most focus on; they are the body parts that most show gender difference and most reveal femininity.

A woman, conversely, won't judge a man's attractiveness on his overt gender signals nearly so much. Instead she concentrates on his personality as shown in face, eyes and body language rather than on his broad shoulders or hairy chest. Penis size can count in bed (though women tend to prefer generosity in width rather than length), but it has little or no bearing on initial attraction.

Weight-wise, slimness may not be nearly as crucial to attractiveness as the media tend to suggest it is. Women can see a well-rounded man as likely to be a good provider, a protector, or an emotional comforter, while only 31 per cent of men in a recent survey said that they preferred slim partners, and older men in particular have been shown to like a body size that is, in fashion terms, on the generous side.

However, if a person's shape is verging on the very large, then they'll come up against a general human prejudice against obesity – even children have been shown to discriminate against plump school friends. The (inaccurate) prejudice nowadays seems to be that while we have no control over our height or our colour, we are able to control our weight – so, if we're not slim, that must mean that we are greedy and lazy.

FASHION SENSE Let's move from body inheritance, over which we have only limited control, to clothes and image, over which we have a great deal. And here let's debunk yet another myth; overtly sexual clothes, such as tight jeans or low necklines, are not the way to find love. They are the way to create arousal in the opposite gender, but relationships are not built on arousal alone – a very sexually obvious fashion statement, for example, can put prospective partners off. And herein lies one of the main differences in approach between men and women when judging a partner's attractiveness. For, although appearance counts for women, it often doesn't nearly as much for men. A woman's sense of style is, to her, a sign of status, intelligence and success.

▶ Men will naturally adopt a different body language from that of women – more erect, more balanced, with a more direct gaze and serious expression.

But many a man doesn't judge image or fashion in this light – he reacts simply to how an outfit strikes his senses, not to the statement it makes. This is why he often chooses clothes that don't do him justice, and why he will often compliment a woman on her appearance when he doesn't think she looks good. What he sees is a particularly appealing shade or texture, while what she is painfully aware of is that the style is three years out of date.

So if it is overall image that appeals to a woman – be that a casual, sophisticated or sexy

image – what appeals to a man when it comes to clothes? Colour is important: some men prefer bright colours, others pastels; yet others prefer rich hues, dull colours, or black and white. Men may also have a preference for contrast or non-contrast – the visual impact of two very different shades or the quieter statement that is made by varying hues of a single colour. They may prefer patterned or plain, shiny or matt, smooth or woolly, satiny or velvety, movement or lack of it in both jewellery and clothes.

The problem here is that these variations don't necessarily indicate which sort of person prefers what type of image. There is a slight preference among extroverts for bright colours, and a slight preference among introverts for dull ones, but beyond that, studies have shown no real correspondence between a person's taste and their personality.

Where this information is useful, though, is in observing the tastes of a particular individual. If they always wear toned-down Fair Isle, then the chances are that sharp black and white will make them wince; if they themselves prefer smart business wear, they'll probably prefer a partner who dresses the same.

There is a natural tendency for couples to match each other in all sorts of ways (see page 80) so, once you are in a relationship, without compromising your own style, you may find yourself choosing clothes that support your partner's likings. But remember, conversely, that the more involved with you a partner becomes, the more they will start to concentrate on those parts of your body that reveal your personality, thoughts and feelings, and the less they will actually notice what you're wearing.

◀ **Women tend to smile more, tilt their heads in an interested way, display legs and body to emphasize length and slimness; this usually means sitting at an angle, which can give the impression of uncertainty.**

ATTRACTION SIGNALS Remember finally, however, that although appearance has impact it is never as important as the more fluid aspects of body language. Within seconds of seeing you, a prospective partner will be much less aware of your looks than of your facial expression, your eye movements, your hand gestures. Within seconds of meeting a person who attracts you, you will be much less aware of his image than of the way he stands, moves or smiles.

So which body language styles attract? Confident body language is certain to work. Even from across the room, someone who moves easily and with a smile, and who has an upright but relaxed posture, will be attractive – simply because onlookers will imagine that positive attitude being focused on them and so will want to make contact.

An equal guarantee of attractiveness is a genuine fascination with what is happening. Few people, men or women, can resist the non-verbal message that wide eyes, a forward lean and approval nods send out, even if these are not being aimed directly at them.

Finally, openness signals are also effective. For it is always a challenge to make social contact, and making contact that may lead to sexual involvement is even more challenging. So whatever you can do to make it easy for others to approach will encourage them towards you.

The basic guidelines for both genders are the same: let your body language show people that you are open and friendly. Keep your shoulders down, your gestures open, your expression warm. Don't pen yourself into a corner, with barriers up in the form of a bag or a chair, but rather make yourself accessible and easily reached. Face 'out' into the room from where you're sitting, look up regularly as if wanting to make eye contact. In short, make anyone within range feel that, were they to approach you, you'd welcome them.

▲ Differing display behaviours, with contradictory messages. Despite the range of positions and expressions, only two of these people are not concerned with making contact; Andrew, second left, and Kay, second right, show by their lack of eye contact that they just aren't interested.

Getting together

When it comes to making contact with a potential partner, it may all seem completely spontaneous. But psychologists have identified a definite courting sequence that takes place, in one form or another, in most situations where people want to explore relationship possibilities.

The first step is to show yourself off. Both men and women do this instinctively in any public situation, even when they're not looking for a partner. So once a woman is aware of attention, she may begin with a general and unconscious show of femininity, sitting up straight to emphasize her breasts or crossing her legs so that her ankles or thighs are seen to best advantage. She may make a display of what she knows to be her own personal best features, flicking her long hair back or turning her head to show her best side. She might 'preen', unconsciously improving her appearance by licking her lips, pulling her dress down and straightening or adjusting jewellery.

▲ Who's interested in whom? Second left, Kay is still shutting out any interest with her expression and blocking arm; far right, Lucy looks polite, but is also less interested in Craig than he is in her. Oliver and Jo's matching positions, smiles and eye contact clearly show their rapport.

Across the room, a male rite will be going on. He will be straightening his back, squaring his shoulders, pulling in his stomach, or adjusting his tie – the equivalent preening behaviour for a man.

And, fascinatingly, once two people start to show off, Nature will lend a helping hand so that both undergo some automatic and uncontrollable body changes to make them look more attractive – such as increased muscle tone, reduced under-eye bagginess and slightly fuller lips.

This classic first phase of courting is not only about signalling 'I'm available', but also 'I'm safe' and 'I'm not going to mess you about'. So if you catch yourself deliberately displaying in a general social situation, it's actually best to tone your movements down.

POINTING If either gender then becomes aware of one particular person they want to attract, they'll move on to the second stage of the courtship sequence, using directional 'pointers' to show that they recognize each other and that they're interested. Without consciously realizing it, you'll make sure that your gaze and your gestures are aimed in the other's direction.

If your interest isn't being returned, your enthusiasm will fade – these body language sequences naturally die if not reciprocated. If it is being returned, however, then you may well end up being more overt than you think. At this stage in the courtship sequence, once you've caught someone's eye, either side may be wary of getting it wrong, and so there's a natural tendency to exaggerate what you're doing to give unambiguous, non-verbal encouragement.

So you may look across, gaze until a potential partner returns your glance, hold eye contact for just a second, look away, then glance back to catch them still looking. To confirm your interest, you may 'point' your gestures, crossing your legs so that a knee or foot is aimed in the right direction, make a gesture that indicates with your hand, finger, knife or fork. He or she, meanwhile, will be doing the same. You'll feel sure that they are interested, though unless you know body language, you may not know why you're sure. If you notice them doing all the things mentioned above, then you can be more certain that your gut reactions are well-founded.

How easy it is to take the next step – making verbal contact – will largely depend on the situation: how crowded the venue, how near you are to each other and how acceptable it is to move around and approach each other. If you're seated on opposite sides of a restaurant, then you'll have to work hard to cross the divide, whereas in a club you need only wait until the other person is dancing and then dance, too.

CHECKING OUT Once you've begun to interact, then you'll both be making a whole new level of assessments. Words will start to matter more as you start to talk – though the topic of conversation will actually be irrelevant – you're sizing each other up and for that body language is still vital.

Initially, you'll both be checking that what you saw from afar is just as good close up. Eyes, mouths, and hands are the parts you'll focus on most, visually scanning quickly and almost constantly with an average of two separate eye movements every second.

Equally, you'll be checking out each other's body rhythms (see page 22). With friends, the key is that your rhythms should match as closely as possible, but with potential lovers it may well be different rhythms that attract. So the other person may feel drawn to you because your easy body posture makes him or her feel comfortable, while you may feel attracted because their speedy style gives you excitement. Although there needs to be underlying matching, perhaps in your posture or voice tone, your body rhythms may, in fact, be complementary rather than identical.

Your sense of smell will also play its part. The closer you get, the more easily you'll be able to pick up each other's personalized body odour signatures. If these don't appeal, then without you even knowing it, your body rhythms will become increasingly mismatched; you'll find it less easy to face each other and keep eye contact. If your odour signatures do appeal, however, the pheromones (chemical substances designed to attract) that they contain will directly affect your nervous system, exciting and arousing you.

Finally, you'll both keep checking each other's responses. Is there mutual liking, are you both available? Here, you have to be careful. Studies show that all men unconsciously use non-verbal 'display' signals when with a woman they desire, even when they have partners, in fact even when those partners are in the same room!

FLIRTING If the information you've gained by being close has made you both even more keen, you may move on to the next step, which is to

▲ **Even a slight shift in body language can indicate shifting interest. Kay has taken pity on Andrew and turned towards him; her eye contact over the glass is a typical flirting gesture. Lucy has dropped her defensive arm and leaned in towards Craig. Centre, Oliver and Jo have moved yet closer.**

flirt. This part of the courtship sequence, which can last for months or even – in the case of some lucky couples – for years, bonds you together non-verbally by bringing you closer, convincing you of the importance of the relationship, and ensuring that no one else intrudes.

The opening move emphasizes all the signals of attraction. You move closer to each other, face each other fully, gaze into each other's eyes and smile. You each find excuses to touch, accentuating your words by a hand on his arm, or passing something across so your fingers meet. Your voices instinctively drop in pitch, become low, soft and husky as they would in love-making. The effect of being so close to each other makes your physical functions react; you not only feel aroused, but also light-headed, as your heart-rate rises and adrenaline pumps around your body.

The second step is almost akin to a retreat, a withdrawal from interaction. Momentarily, one of you will withdraw all the attention they've been giving: turning away to pick up a glass, reacting to something in the distance, avoiding eye contact, masking your face or eyes behind your hand. The prospective partner may respond with a similar withdrawal and, for just a second, you'll both seem to lose the closeness you had, and your bodies may respond with a burst of anxiety, so that you reach out for each other again with relief. It all helps convince you both non-verbally that this relationship is something you don't want to let go of.

And, just to make sure there's no threat to your relationship, one or both of you will also put up 'block off' signals to discourage intruders. When you very first meet, it tends to be the man alone who gives these in an obvious, physical way, placing his body so that it effectively bars entry to any would-be newcomer. After a few meetings, though, the woman will start blocking, too, in more subtle ways, keeping the man's attention on her by her eye contact or laughter, a light touch or a kiss if at any time his eye is tempted to wander.

Most of these non-verbal flirting techniques are so natural that any conscious attempt at improvement would spoil them. What you can do is to be aware of them and enjoy them – they are instinctive ways of attracting a mate, not un-liberated manipulations. Your partner's external signals will show whether they're enjoying what is happening, and your own internal signs will tell you whether you are happy with how things are progressing. Pull back a little if they're going too fast; encourage them with a smile if you like something they've done or said.

Through these non-verbal strategies, you can keep each other involved for sufficient time to assess the possibilities fully. If you aren't convinced, you'll say your goodbyes and go. And if you each suspect that the other isn't convinced – because you see their body position shifting, their eye contact wavering, and their gestures signalling that they've spotted someone else across the room – then give up gracefully and turn your attention elsewhere.

SEDUCTION When both you and he are ready to move your relationship on to an intimate level, you'll need to set the time and the place. Make sure you do so in a way that non-verbally as well as verbally creates the best chance of success.

As far as timing is concerned, evening is still probably the best time to begin intimacy. Not only are people more open to close interaction when they have time to relax at the end of a working day, but research has shown that increasing darkness encourages us to look and touch rather than speak. In one study of a group in a dark room, talking died away completely after about half an hour. So, clichéd though it is, the classic romantic venue of a dimly lit restaurant may best put your bodies in the mood.

Choose a location where you're naturally placed close together. Human bodies are actually programmed to make the leap from physical closeness to sexual intimacy. Once within the 'intimate' distance zone of 46 cm (18 in), you're far more likely to have sexual contact. And as this contact is also typically preceded by a 'spontaneous' or 'excuse' touch, you may also want to opt for a small restaurant table to make it more likely that you'll accidentally brush hands.

Choose a place that has music to make it more possible that your rhythms will come into synchrony, though not somewhere where there's audience participation – you want all attention focused inwards to each other, not outwards to the room. In the same way, try to arrange the setting for built-in block-offs as described earlier on this page, for example, a pillar to shield you from other diners, or a table well away from the distraction of the kitchen door.

Once the evening's public activity is over, then – unless your partner feels uncomfortable away from their own territory – it's best (and of course, safest) to end up at your place. There you can plan the environment for accessibility plus reassurance. Make sure there's somewhere that you can comfortably sit together with the potential to move closer, though if your private space contains only a bed then take care; it can

▲ 'Keep off' is the clear signal here. His route to her is made inaccessible with a table on the floor and cushions on the sofa. The telephone in full view signals that she's available for interruptions. The lights are full on. Despite her small smile, these signals, along with her slight backward tilt, tensely twisted legs, crossed arms and averted gaze should give him the obvious message to keep his distance.

▶ Her non-verbal message in this situation is very different. She's removed any physical blocks or possible distractions, and turned the lights down. She's turned directly towards him, 'pointed' with knee and foot, and met his gaze in a way that clearly signals she wants to move closer.

▲ They've narrowed the distance and initiated an 'accidental' touch in the way she pours the wine.

feel too close to sex for comfort, and your bodies may create compensatory barriers by becoming tense and wary.

Throughout, allow yourselves to move away from the senses of sight and sound and on to the more sensual channels of touch, smell and taste. So remove all distractions, such as the phone or the housemates. Introduce traditional elements with a deserved reputation for enhancing sex: low lights, deep music, soft cushions. But again, don't overdo things with overtly sexual mood music or scene-setting. If either of you feels unsafe, you'll find it more difficult to become aroused.

TAKING THE LEAD Soon you'll be ready for some serious touching. You'll probably have touched before – it's very unusual to move straight from no contact directly to full sexual intimacy. You'll both have tested out the water with 'excuse' touches, and these will have proved encouraging: your smell, taste and feel will have appealed; you'll both have moved forward rather than back; your skin will have felt warm rather than cold to the touch. If all goes well, at this point your own instinctive body language strategies will take over.

But what if you don't both spontaneously leap into each other's arms? Could it be that you are simply not attracted to each other? If either of you keep showing all the signs of a friendship (see pages 38–9), ease back to the other end of the sofa and take things more slowly. If one of you is showing signs of distraction, such as pulling back, looking away, or trying to talk rather than look – then quite simply back off. If it's you who are distracted, then turn the lights up and clearly and cleanly communicate that you don't want to take things further.

What if your partner is returning all your display and flirtation signs, but things just aren't progressing the way you want? Maybe they are wary of going further. Maybe you have misread the signs and they haven't really registered your non-verbal interest. You can take the initiative in a number of ways. Though be warned; these are not manipulative strategies but forms of encouragement. They are simply intended to speed up the natural process of physical intimacy and if either of you is seriously uninterested, none of them will work.

Move closer – as mentioned before, being within the 46 cm (18 in) intimacy zone is a clear signal from you to him (or vice versa) that you are happy to make intimate contact. Increase the frequency of those accidental touches, which normally precede sexual contact: look at something together so that they have to sit close to you. When your hands do meet, make sure they know that the touch is not accidental, and that you are aroused by it.

You'll already have noticed the ways in which the two of you are posturally or gesturally matching or mirroring each other. So, as you match posture, move a little closer. If the other person is attracted to you, they'll be naturally encouraged to respond. As you mirror their gesture, allow your hand to linger, inviting further touch. Lean well forward when gazing into their eyes, or lift your head when you cuddle up. Whisper something loving; they'll automatically lean closer in order to hear and, when your lips meet, it will be totally natural to take things just that stage further.

SEXUAL CODES Surely once you've kissed, you can forget body language. But if anything, knowing and responding to body language is even more vital during sex than at any other time as words are often more difficult to use then. And, no matter how many sex manuals you read, remember there are no rules. Everyone is an individual. What works for one person may turn another off, and what works for someone on one occasion may be a sexual disaster next time.

Where body language is vital is that it provides a series of non-verbal codes with which you naturally communicate your level of arousal. Successful couples tend to develop these codes instinctively, but many partners either don't become aware of them, or fail to respond to and reinforce them.

These codes have their basis in your natural arousal mechanisms. As you become sexually excited, your bodies undergo a dramatic change. Her breasts become firm, the areola swelling and the nipples becoming erect. Her uterus expands and lifts, her clitoris hardens and engorges, her vagina plumps up, filling with blood in readiness to hold his penis. Meanwhile, his penis erects as it becomes filled with blood, his testicles swell and his body prepares for ejaculation.

You each experience these major physiological changes as passion, and manifest them not only through your genitals, but also through the whole of the rest of your body. Your lips and skin, for example, fill with blood while your nerve endings become much more sensitive; your eyes mist over and lose focus, and your hearing sensitivity diminishes so as to allow you to concentrate on what's happening inside rather than outside. Your muscle tone also changes, often causing a trembling or a softening of your skin, which may in turn flush and become moist. In addition, your facial expression may shift, perhaps becoming more contorted, or you may lose expression completely as your body becomes

▲ They are starting to become intimate but maybe they're not sure. His tense back and leg angle – almost trying to turn away – signals wariness, while their open eyes show they can't abandon themselves completely to sensation as yet.

▲ Their mouth-to-mouth kissing signals the start of real intimacy and trust. It has its roots in the mouth-to-mouth feeding that mother apes give to babies when weaning. The next step, using tongues as in 'French kissing', is even more sexual because it replicates the act of penetration.

overwhelmed with sensation. Your voice may soften, and become deeper and more husky. Your breathing may change as your heart-rate rises and adrenaline pumps around your body. Your smell and taste may alter, too; the sebaceous glands at the edge of your lips and mouth will produce chemicals that signal your arousal, and your genitals will change their odour as you near orgasm.

All these signals, both the conscious and the unconscious ones, form part of a sexual code, a constant stream of high-quality information that both of you give and receive, that allows you to tell each other what's good and what is less good, what you want more of and what less, what is working and what isn't. You may not even be aware of giving or receiving these sexual codes, but they dictate the whole pace – and pleasure – of your love-making.

You can, of course, do nothing to affect the unconscious codes that each of you uses, the shifts in heart-rate, blood pressure, smell or taste that are outside your control. Where you can enhance love-making, though, is by paying attention to your more conscious codes, making sure that both of you know and understand what they mean. Your movement codes – a sudden stillness or an urgent thrusting – carry the messages 'Go on' or 'Stop'. Your sound codes – a murmur or a sharp intake of breath – may indicate that something is more or less pleasurable. Touch codes, such as a fingertip pressure or an urgent hand, guide position, movement and speed. You can become aware of them in yourself, and make them clearer and more specific; you can become aware of them in your partner, learn what precisely they mean and how best to respond. You can become

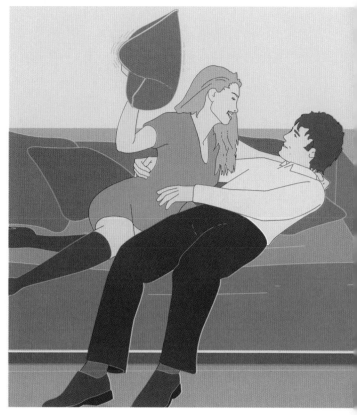

▲ ▸ Mock fighting allows them to touch, raises their physical energy and increases body adrenaline – arousing them still further.

familiar with the subtlest gradations of your sexual codes, so that even the slightest of movements from one of you will allow the other to respond in the most arousing way.

There may be two particular difficulties with using these codes to become more in tune through sex. First, one partner may not seem to register the other's signals. This is particularly true with men, who can get so lost in their own arousal that they hardly register their partner's non-verbal requests. If this happens, simply exaggerate your signs until the other responds and, if you absolutely have to, add an instant verbal translation by saying, 'Yes … more' so that he really gets the message and remembers it in future. Don't worry, incidentally, about signalling when you don't like something – the most effective way to do this is simply to let your positive sounds, movements and touches stop.

Second, one of you may find it difficult to show obvious signs of arousal. This is as likely to be the man as the woman, for despite the male complaint that women don't 'show they're enjoying it', men equally often fail to provide useful non-verbal signals when making love; years of being in control means that it may seem unimportant to signal what's good, because often they can arrange things to suit themselves. So a woman may have to take the initiative and find out what her partner likes. It's a sex-manual cliché to remind her to spend time touching him fully with hand and mouth as part of making love, but in bodytalk terms this manoeuvre has several important advantages: it arouses the nerves so that the skin engorges, thereby creating a larger area available for touching; it brings all the senses into play; and it allows her to find out what pleases.

▲ Their undressing each other signals real intent on both sides. So does their instinctive response to being undressed: moving closer in a way that makes the job easier shows willingness. If they had pulled away, that would have indicated that removing clothes is too far a step to undertake right now.

Perhaps the most difficult thing about using body language in bed is that with a new partner you should begin to communicate non-verbally right from the very first time you touch. Let the other person hear your sounds and feel your movements from the first time you kiss. Start to become aware of what their touches and murmurs mean from the very first time. Although this may sound like an unromantic thing to do, if you leave it until the second time, it will almost be too late. This is because you and your partner are most receptive at the start of a relationship. If you each signal clearly what you really like at that point, you'll be setting the agenda from the beginning and will later be able to expand the possibilities. If you don't signal clearly, it will become more and more difficult to 're-instruct' each other as your relationship progresses.

In time, as you continue to develop your love-making, you'll learn all each other's codes – those that allow you to help each other towards climax, to hold each other just short of climax, to tip each other over into an extended orgasm. The good news is that the more you observe, interpret and respond to their signals, and the more they are able to respond to yours, the more expert you'll become and the more enjoyable sex will be.

Emotional body language

Our human bodies are programmed to have emotions, to signal – both internally and externally – when something wonderful happens and when something awful happens. A love relationship will almost certainly include both of these extremes of feeling.

It's relatively easy to spot when either you or your partner is overwhelmed with emotion, particularly the 'classic six' emotions that have the same body language all over the world, from Japan to Argentina: happiness, sadness, anger, disgust, surprise, fear. You'll signal happiness to each other through your smiles; sadness through your tears; anger through your raised voices or strong gestures. (However, you may never see real fear in each other unless you're involved in a traumatic incident together.)

Where real body language skill emerges, however, is not in spotting these obvious signs of emotion, but in noticing the much more subtle manifestations of feeling that everyone experiences every day. Satisfaction, regret, irritation, distaste, confusion and anxiety are the toned-down versions of the full-blown feelings. If you are able to spot the signs of these in yourself and your partner early on, you'll be well equipped to cope with them in you both.

The first sign of an emotion you may well notice in yourself will be some kind of internal rush of energy. This is because emotions were originally designed as a way of resourcing you to cope with an outside threat, as well as signalling to others in your 'tribe' that you needed help with whatever was affecting you.

Emotions are real physical events, just like hunger or thirst, with your entire autonomic nervous system moving into action. On the inside, adrenaline pours into your bloodstream, your heart-beat and blood pressure soar, your breathing rate rises, your nervous system is flooded with sugar to give you energy, your digestive system slows down so as not to waste that energy, and your coagulation rate falls in case there's blood spilled.

Parallel to this, each particular emotion will have its own specific effect within your body. Anxiety might make itself felt by a churning in your stomach that is so common that it is has a special word in English – 'butterflies'. You may also get tightness down the centre line of your body, a faster heart-beat, a dry mouth, a slightly cold sensation, and perhaps a sudden need to go to the toilet. If you are experiencing regret, you'll feel your eyes prickle, a vague precursor of tears; your nose or throat may feel slightly blocked, and there'll typically be a heavy feeling down your centre line. The earliest sign of irritation may be a sudden tingling, a movement in your stomach, a rushing in your head or hands, a sudden clenching of your jaw.

Be aware of your emotions as you feel them day-by-day. That way, you not only gain more communication with your own body, literally encouraging it to 'tell' you when it thinks there is something to be wary of or angry about. You also have more chance of responding to your emotions, which is a skill useful not only in love relationships but also throughout your life.

HIS FEELINGS A special note here on men's emotions. It's often difficult to read a man's emotional body language. Traditionally, men in our society aren't encouraged to be in touch with their feelings. The most commonly displayed male emotion is anger and that's often the one they express in order to relieve the internal stress of all the physical events described above. (Very often, in fact, their real, underlying feeling may be one of grief or fear.)

An anxious man will have typical frowning worry lines on his forehead (in apes, this signals a desire to escape from something but not being able to). His shoulders may be raised, as if in

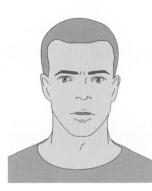

FOUR BASIC EMOTIONS SHOW VERY DIFFERENT SIGNS.

◄ FEAR When we feel fear, our eyes open and stare; its original, primitive function was to help us see the threat better. Eyebrows rise and draw together in protection, and lips are drawn back as if in a scream. A woman is more likely to turn away and to the side, while a man will draw back but face the threat.

◄ GRIEF Even before we start to cry, our eyelids lower and redden as the tears approach. Our head drops, and often our whole body follows suit, as if to protect ourselves as we mourn. Our lower lip trembles as if we feel like howling with grief.

◄ ANGER We try to stare down the opposition with a penetrating gaze, draw our eyebrows together and flare our nostrils. A man may push his lips forward, as if he is in preparation for a threatening yell, while a woman, more used to holding back her anger, may instead press her lips together to stop the sound.

◄ HAPPINESS The positive version of anger, this emotion prepares us for celebratory action. Our eyes open wide to see better, our head goes up with ears 'pricked' to hear better. A genuine smile is usually wide, showing the teeth and involving the muscles around the eyes.

protection, and he may tend to hunch forward instead of sitting normally. He'll often bite his lip or move his mouth – almost as if he's trying to talk through the problem in his head.

And, while men often find it difficult to cry, one who is feeling regretful or sad may well show redness or puffiness around the eyes, with a gleam of moisture along the lower eyelid. His mouth will tremble slightly, his body slumping and, without really being aware that he is doing so, he may sigh heavily.

An irritated man, meanwhile, will tend to stare with lowered brows, as if staring down an opponent before an attack. His nose may flare, his lips tighten, his shoulders hunch, his movements get short and sharp or uncoordinated. His colour may change, so that his face turns white or red, as his nervous system alternately makes him angry and then tries to calm him down.

But what if he's experiencing conflicting emotions – angry at his partner but scared of her response; resentful that she walked out but relieved that she's back? It's vital for a woman to spot signs of such contradictory emotion, because if she doesn't, she may handle things in the wrong way, reacting to the single emotion she thinks she sees rather than to the other emotion that the man is also feeling.

So both men and women need to watch out for conflicting signals. These signals typically occur in zones, with one emotion appearing in one zone while a different reaction occurs in another. Scientists speculate that this happens because different parts of the brain are instructing different parts of the body. Typical 'contradiction zones' are: top half of body versus bottom half (for example, tears on the face but irritated foot taps); top half of face versus bottom half (smile to reassure you, but fear in his eyes); left half of body versus right half (tilting head or shifting shoulders and hands); whole body versus single gesture (a relaxed posture and loving expression plus

clenched fist). And, of course, don't forget to check for body language that actually contradicts the words: a peaceful statement but an angry mouth, a loving phrase but a withdrawn hand.

Letting it out

The boss shouts, the train is late or, on a more serious level, there's a redundancy or a bereavement. Whether it's you that's feeling bad or it's your partner, you may feel that the most helpful and loving way to behave is to be cheerful and encourage them to be the same.

However, from a body language point of view, the opposite is often true. For when we continuously push down our feelings, we put our bodies in a double bind. If we constantly feel sad, anxious or irritated – and then, as a result, constantly put the brakes on these emotions – our natural control mechanisms will go into overdrive, and the result can be to keep our bodies on a see-saw of stress. Medical research now suggests that this kind of emotional suppression can lead to all kinds of long-term problems, including heart disease, cancer and depression. So rather than keeping a stiff upper lip, a more useful and successful way of handling your body responses may well be to ventilate the emotion, thus letting your body off the hook.

How can you best do this? Check this out with each other, for needs differ between people and individuals want different kinds of support. But if either of you is anxious or sad, then almost always a whole body hug is the best way to offer comfort – it reminds your body non-verbally of when you were very small and totally protected, and so makes you feel safe and loved. Hold each other firmly, closely and without any attempt at sexuality, feeling your breathing and heart-rates start to match reassuringly.

If either of you is angry, then often exercise helps, by using up the adrenaline that the body produces. Running can be good; hitting a cushion can feel better. Make your movements strong and powerful and breathe steadily while you move. If your house is soundproof, don't be afraid to shout while you're doing it; if it isn't, bury your head in the cushions to scream. If you can, flail or shout in supportive unison; but if it's each other you're feeling bad about, do all the above by yourselves, meeting up only when you're feeling better. (And whatever the source of the anger, if the emotion keeps coming back, seek outside help.)

Once you sense that you've expressed all your emotion, and are spontaneously starting to feel better, use the following non-verbal sequence to key back into normal life. Get to your feet and move around, with your head up and eyes slightly raised to the ceiling. Breathe deeply and slowly. Do some kind of complex but non-risky physical activity such as wiggling your toes one by one, which will allow the nervous system to start using some of its energy. Then do some kind of complex but undemanding mental activity, such as counting the ceiling tiles, which will turn your attention away from any residual emotional signals you may be experiencing.

This sequence can also work if you need to act naturally when you're feeling bad. It will help if you have no opportunity to express your emotion and will carry you through until you can deal with the problem properly. But like all the suggestions in this section, it isn't the solution to deep emotional trauma, serious relationship conflict or long-term depression, for which you need on-going support or professional counselling.

Problems, problems

When problems strike your partnership, the answer in many cases involves the use of words. You talk through difficulties, you discuss them with others, you visit a counsellor and speak to him or her about them. Where body language helps is, first, by alerting you to a problem and, second, by making sure that the words are most

effective. And, just occasionally, there are body language solutions to your problems.

What can you do if, for example, you suspect your partner might be deceiving you? Their body language won't tell you exactly what the lie might be or what the truth is; but it can help you clarify whether there's a problem.

If your partner's lying, they won't want you to spot what they're really feeling; their initial tactic may be instinctively to reduce their non-verbal signals. So look first for 'blanking signs' – being quieter and somehow more still than usual, with gestures and expressions toned down, fewer eyebrow flashes and a tense mouth and jaw as they keep control.

Or they may show you a false front, with a loving expression. But check the smile. A genuine one is balanced, one side of the face to the other, with wrinkles round the eyes; a false one is unsymmetrical, stronger on the left side of the face (in right-handed people), with no eye wrinkles and a fixed, slowly fading expression. If they're trying to stop themselves telling you something, they may stutter, trip over their words, use the 'choker' gesture with their hand to their throat, or talk through their fingers as if trying to block off their voice.

To see behind this masking behaviour, look at those parts of their body that they have less control over than the face or hands. You may spot 'escape' movements of legs or feet, tension in the shoulders or stomach. They may non-verbally comfort themselves, by touching their face, smoothing their hair, or 'wringing' their hands. Their breathing may be uneven, with little stops and jerks, their skin colour may change, and they may perspire and blink more than usual.

So what can you do? You can never get a partner to tell you what they don't want to, but a simple body language technique can make it clear to you both that something is being hidden. If you want to challenge them, do so in private

and when you're close. Position yourself so that your partner has to face you directly, lean forward and hold their hands to stop the nervous movements that give them release from inner tension. Look into their eyes, which will make it difficult for them to control their emotions. Make your voice soft rather than angry, which will stop them hiding their guilty body language under resentful non-verbal signals.

If they squirm and wriggle, if they cannot meet your eyes, and if all their nervous body language signals increase, then there is a problem and that fact will be clear to both of you – though how you then handle things is up to you. If, on the other hand, your partner stays calm, relaxes into your gaze and sighs, then they may simply be a supremely good liar. The chances are, however, that your worries are really for nothing.

▲ WHO IS REALLY WITH WHOM?
In the scene above, the real attraction is between Lisa and Richard on the left, whose positioning and eye contact clearly show their interest in each other. Richard's 'pointers' of head and knee are to Lisa – even though his arms and hands point back to his real partner, Kate, sitting on the sofa. Richard blocks what's happening from Kate with his body angle.

SUSPICIOUS MINDS Any suspicion of deceit automatically becomes more upsetting if you suspect that what your partner is deceiving you about is an affair. How can you tell and what, if anything, can you do about that?

If the possible 'other woman or other man' isn't part of your circle, then in all honesty an intelligent partner can often hide this secret successfully if they want to. The clichéd non-

▶ When Kate challenges Richard with a touch in the second picture, as you see here, he turns sharply and defensively to her. Does Kate need to worry? Richard's body is giving contradictory evidence, so maybe she ought to keep an eye on him.

verbal signals such as a new perfume lingering in the car or love bites on her neck are so common-place that both your partner and their lover will avoid them carefully.

What should alert your suspicions, however, is any change in a partner's non-verbal approach towards you. And that, interestingly enough, holds true whether the change is for the better or for the worse. For example, a sudden and unexplained drop in the amount you see your partner is bad news. But it may not be entirely good news if there is a sudden increase in the amount you make love – it may mean that your partner's libido has been stimulated by their new lover so they want more sex in general – including from you. If you're in a long-term relationship then watch out for a sudden drop in your bonding signals, such as eye contact and forward leans. But also be aware of the introduction of any new non-verbal sequences, such as taking your arm instead of holding your hand, or snuggling up on the sofa or in bed in a way that is different from usual. For while your partner may well be able to stop telling you about a new affair, they will find it much more difficult to prevent the new bonding behaviours they're learning with their lover from creeping into their repertoire with you.

If you suspect that your rival is someone from your circle of friends, you do have more chance to find out the truth because you can watch them together. If an affair is just building and hasn't started yet, you may see all the normal display signals from your partner – grooming behaviours, display behaviours and flirting. If your suspected rival responds (see page 57), then you do have cause to worry.

If you suspect that an affair has already started, watch out, too, for a lack of rapport between your partner and your rival. Be as suspicious of that as you would be of increased rapport – for if 'he' stops looking at 'her', stops smiling at her, removes all expression from his voice when he talks to her and keeps a bigger distance between

them than he would have before, then he has something he needs to hide. Check such an unusual shift in behaviour by looking at your partner's unconscious signals; if their postural matching and unconscious 'directional pointers' of hand, knee and shoulder (see pages 59–60) are still towards you, then there may well not be a problem. If, however, your partner's non-verbal signals are all directed at their potential lover, the time has probably come for you to stop observing and start acting – challenging your partner, talking through the problems and creating a situation in which both their words and gestures are focused solely and genuinely on you.

▲ A smouldering row is signalled by his angry expression – here the forward lean shows anger rather than interest. She turns away and does not meet his gaze – a typical way to keep a row under wraps. Her tension and anxiety are shown by her folded hands while his are held loosely as if ready for attack.

▲ Here, her anger shows more. Her more directly facing posture and gaze signals that she is squaring up to him; her hands are now parted as if for action rather than for protection. He, though, has returned his hands to his pockets – non-verbally aiming to reassure her that he's less liable to attack.

PUTTING THE BRAKES ON Whether at the start of a relationship or at any time during it, you may feel the need to slow things down sexually or emotionally. Your partner wants to go further, to sleep with you or to marry you; you want to stop and take your time.

The problem is that in this type of situation it is extremely tempting simply to 'be nice' to your partner. This fact often makes women, in particular, use body language that appears much more pleasant and agreeable than we feel inside. So even when we say 'No', we often accompany it

with a reassuring half-smile or head nod, as if to say, 'It's all right'. Unfortunately, what a partner may think we're really saying is, 'If you keep asking, eventually I'll say yes'.

The key to avoiding this kind of misunderstanding is assertive body language. If you feel that you're being pressured over something, begin by breaking any physical contact and moving back slightly, so you're not tempted to undermine your message by a loving pat or sudden clutch. Face your partner directly and look them in the eye – a sign that you really mean what you're saying. And to make your non-verbal communication even clearer, relax by taking a deep breath and letting it go slowly.

Don't smile, even slightly, as this is the one body signal that undermines a 'No' more than any other. Instead, let your mouth fall into a relaxed but serious position, and drop your chin just slightly so that your throat is open and your voice won't sound 'little-girlish'. Swallow, so that when you do speak you don't begin with a hesitation or stutter, and then talk slowly and briefly. Say what you want to say, and then stop. (Assertiveness teachers often recommend that for maximum effectiveness, you decide what your message is in just a few words and then, if pressured, simply repeat this message rather than adding any explanations or qualifications.)

This style of body language won't give you a totally easy ride, because however calmly you present your case, you're denying your partner what they want, and they'll resent that. But this approach will avoid the endless rounds of discussion and argument that can often happen because they hope that your negative answer is really a positive one in disguise.

What if the reverse is happening, and your partner is saying no to you? How should you respond? First, if they actually use the word 'no', then, whatever their body language, accept what they are saying just as you would want them to if you said it. Ignore body signs; they may well be signalling apology, placation, guilt or fear, all of which will confuse the message.

But what if your partner says yes and you suspect they mean no? Check carefully for ways in which their body is really signalling a negative to you, like minute shakes of the head or wagging of the fingers. Notice hesitations in speech, swallowed phrases or false starts that indicate that what they want to say is something very different from what they're actually saying. Reading the real meaning on both verbal and

non-verbal channels may not remove conflict, but it will make communication clearer and, in the long run, create a better resolution.

It's over now

You may think that if you feel nerve-wrackingly anxious when your partner rings, or furious when you see them, your relationship is in deep trouble. In fact, though it undoubtedly is bad news, it may not be the worst. For if feeling is still there, then you still have an emotional bond; your body still considers this relationship to be important. The relationship may be a painful one, but it is not over.

On the other hand, if what you experience when you phone or meet them is merely a slight sinking feeling or an anaesthetized sensation, then your body may be telling you that this relationship is now of no significance in your life. It may well be time to move away.

If you still feel something, but your partnership is hitting problems, check out your mutual body language. A long-term relationship may not show the in-love signs of a new one, so don't worry if these signs are not there. Do worry, however, if your partner moves back as you move forward or vice versa, if you can no longer meet each other's eyes, if you're mismatching and tripping over each other in words and movements. All this means that you are no longer in non-verbal synchrony.

Next, check the energy level between you. A viable relationship will create vitality (except in cases of short-term exhaustion), giving your movements vigour and your voice tone strength. If, when you're around each other, your energy level drops completely, your posture and gestures are tired and slumped, your faces and voices devoid of expression, then there is little stimulation left in your partnership.

Check, too, those most basic of emotional barometers: taste and smell. In a dying relationship, you often suddenly find that these are distasteful. You may think that your partner's

▲ Here, her lowered head shows agreement and acquiescence, a tribal signal of wanting to bring a conflict to an end. But her pouting lips show that she is still angry; things have not really been resolved.

suddenly developed bad breath, when the fact is that their body odour signature hasn't changed; it just doesn't appeal to you any more.

Finally, check out your sexuality. A drop in the frequency you make love is natural in a long-term relationship, and may also happen temporarily if either of you are under stress. But a distaste for love-making, a shrinking away from touch or a lack of sexual response, even once you get going, is your body's way of telling you that there's definitely something wrong.

Can body language help to reverse the process? Most of the signals mentioned above are symptoms of an underlying problem, not causes. They reflect the fact that you and your partner have incompatible goals, that you have lost faith in each other, that you've become interested in other people. So trying to change the body language won't work, though if you're able to talk things through and resolve them, then, as if by magic, your non-verbal signs will become positive once more. The one exception to this is where your problems are due to physical incompatibility. You want more cuddles, he does not; he wants sex this way, you want it that way. In this situation, particularly if you get the help of a qualified sex therapist, you can work to realign your body language, both in bed and out of it.

What if you decide to split up? Then, the struggle between you will mostly be in words – the negotiation of the break-up, the discussion of who gets what. But once the final decision is made, you can ease the split by ensuring that you don't give out unhelpful non-verbal signals. When you have to meet, try to avoid communicating your irritation with tense shoulders, a constant frown, tight lips, confrontational eye contact or a sharp voice. Faced with these signals, the human body instinctively moves into attack mode and you'll find your partner becoming increasingly hostile to you, so do your best to keep calm.

On the other hand, offer too many positive signals, and you'll give the non-verbal impression that you're interested again. So make sure that, when you meet, you keep enough distance between you. Erect barriers – a restaurant table or an office desk – and if you sit down, choose a chair that has arms. Make a clear no-go area around you with your gestures, your lack of eye contact, and with a slight frown if your partner approaches. Give the clear message that you want to be on your own and you will avoid any unhappy attempts at reconciliation.

Is it love?

If you are fortunate, then your sexuality will be based on real affection, and your commitment will be based on love.

It may seem as if what we in the Western world call 'love' has nothing to do with the body's behaviour. Surely it's all pure emotion – or, more cynically, nothing more than a fairytale dream? In fact, recent research has shown that the phenomenon is based on actual physiological responses that the body makes to meeting and bonding with another person. When you first set eyes on someone and there's an immediate attraction, your whole body responds. Your brain releases a chemical called phenylethylamine. This has the same effect on your nervous system as any powerful addictive substance – you get high. You become increasingly aware of your own body and its arousal, you are in a state of constant desire. You may lose your appetite, be unable to sleep, suffer adrenaline bursts that make you restless and absent-minded, have an irregular heart-beat and blood pressure. These effects are not all in your mind; they really exist, they really affect your body, they are really triggered by your loved one, and they really are there in order to bring you together.

How you cope with these symptoms depends entirely on your situation. If you're both free and able to fall in love, then you can follow your instincts. You can start creating a bond with your partner in all the wonderfully romantic ways that are so typical of falling in love. Expect to be a little scatterbrained, to have lots of energy, to feel overwhelmingly good; your brain is drip-feeding your body the love drug and as long as that lasts, you'll feel different.

But what if you or the person you love can't form a reciprocal relationship, or having formed one, can't make it work? Then what you experience can be very painful, because your body is suffering an overdose and there seems to be no way of relieving the symptoms. The most useful way to approach this problem is actually nothing to do with body language or with non-verbal communication – it is to become disillusioned with your desired partner as quickly as you can, by whatever means you can. Then, your brain will naturally stop producing phenylethylamine. After a few weeks or months of 'withdrawal symptoms' and 'convalescence', where you feel exhausted and weepy, you'll wake up one day feeling normal again.

Being in love

If your relationship develops, then after a few weeks or a few months, your body will register that there is now no longer any need to push you towards a partnership. A new set of chemicals is released into your brain, this time enkephalins, which help you disregard difficulties and literally deaden any pain you may feel. You begin to feel calm inside, as if sedated – as indeed, to some extent, you are. Your appetite returns, and you start sleeping again. You feel energetic but not frenetic, relaxed and happy.

Your relationship is probably going well. If you have a row or suffer some disillusionment with your partner, you can handle this eventuality because the enkephalins help you do so. As in the first phase of friendship (see page 40), you are learning all about each other, verbally and non-verbally. You still feel sexual, but not as urgently, so although you still make love, you're not desperate if you don't do so.

Your natural non-verbal bonding mechanism is working well – and here's the danger. For it is very easy while you're in this phase to make a commitment based on how you feel rather than on actual compatibility. Success here lies in the ability to overrule your body language; in this situation, it may be misleading. Instead, think through such hard-headed issues as underlying beliefs, common attitudes and life goals. Only if these things fit should you make any commitment.

Strengthening love

If your relationship continues, then at some point – and this could be anything from several months to several years after you've initially met – a third chemical change in your brain occurs. The enkephalins continue, to allow you to cope with any difficulties, but added to them is a dose of endorphins, which make you feel intense pleasure and long-term contentment.

Inside, you feel peaceful, relaxed and content, and your non-verbal communication with your partner tells you that all is well with the relationship. You may, of course, face the occasional problem, but you can still cope with it. And as a result you are able to start turning your attention out to other areas of your life: re-establishing contact with friends, raising your children or building your career.

Seen from the outside, your relationship starts to look more like a friendship than a sexual relationship. The first signals of sexual intimacy, the eye contact, touch and block-offs that signalled 'Keep clear, we're busy' to other people are irrelevant now; you don't need them for reassurance, and other people don't need them in order to know that you're a couple.

You'll be matching, though, on levels deeper than any but the most intimate friendships. You'll not only be matching posture, mirroring gestures, reflecting voice tones and phrases and taking up the same breathing and heart-rate rhythms, you'll also have developed your own non-verbal 'traditions'. These are little sequences of behaviour that are particular to you – ways of gazing, ways of turn-taking, ways of kissing, ways even of rowing that only you two do together. Through all this matching, you may even have developed similar physical weaknesses or susceptibilities: a large number of married couples tend to die of the same disease. Non-verbally, your body language will look to an outsider like a dance without words.

▲ Once a couple bond, their body language may seem to be less similar – but the deep rapport means that even a mock fight shows evidence of body matching.

Staying in love

What if all this doesn't happen? The bottom line is that if a relationship doesn't, over time, develop this kind of deep-level communication, then it may well come to an end. And, as has been stressed earlier, using body language to help an ailing relationship or to bolster a dying one is usually trying to do too little, too late.

What is true, though, is that you can use body language techniques to maintain your love and safeguard your relationship. From the start, keep one eye and one ear on your matching sequences, and provide opportunities to develop them. Do things together that demand you learn what each other's body language patterns are, such as playing sport, or making love, which is the ultimate matching activity. Work so that you become aware of your own and your partner's non-verbal codes, both in bed and out of it, and constantly refine your recognition and understanding of these codes.

Ultimately, if all goes well with your relationship, and your mutual life helps you to understand each other more on a mental level and support each other more on an emotional level, then your body language will follow suit.

4 office life

Whatever your career goals, body language will help you succeed in them. As well as your qualifications, experience and performance, people will, often unconsciously, be judging you on other factors – whether you appear non-verbally confident, competent and efficient.

The body language of the workplace

This section of the book explores work situations: dress code and how best to play the system; how to use body language to feel good at work; and the ways in which body language can help you cope with both your colleagues and your superiors. It then goes on to look at three specific work scenarios – the meeting, the client and the interview. And finally this part of the book shows how, as you continue up the career ladder, body language can help you fulfil your potential and achieve your goals.

Making an impression

What you wear at work makes an individual statement about you. It could be a way of saying to your boss that you're ready for promotion or, to your colleagues, that you're a friendly person; it could be an assertion to a client that you know what you're talking about. So it's wise to think about your agenda and choose your clothes accordingly – and, for a woman, that includes your accessories, make-up and hairstyle as well.

Is it important, for example, for you to be seen to have power and authority, perhaps because you want to influence a client or be taken seriously as a freelancer? The days of power-shoulders are over, but the fact still remains that if you want to appear powerful, both genders have to adopt some of the non-verbal icons of masculinity. For women, the key lies in shape and colour, picking up on the slightly tailored look that is reminiscent of a man's suit, in co-ordinated outfits, using dark or toned-down shades, with light make-up and a simple hairstyle without too many feminine curls.

Say, on the other hand, that you want to create a co-operative, rapportful relationship at work – perhaps because your job involves a good deal of one-to-one interaction or support. Then you need to choose clothes that reflect more feminine emblems – such as lighter, brighter colours, patterned rather than plain materials, and unstructured shapes that signal relaxation and an accepting nature. Women can also use make-up to accentuate those parts of the face that are most expressive – eyes and lips; but keep the colours toned down so as not to slide over the boundary between femininity and sexuality.

▲ Business uniform: for men, the suit, shirt and tie combination seems totally standard – but acceptable shape, material and pattern may vary from company to company. Women have many more choices for clothes – though in traditional professions they often copy the male suit in almost every detail.

▲ Very casual wear, as pictured here, is not acceptable in many work situations. Nevertheless, it is a 'uniform' for leisure activities. Jeans, in particular, have been a casual uniform ever since they became a fashion icon for the 1960s youth culture. They may even be acceptable career wear if teamed with a more formal jacket.

STYLE STATEMENTS You may need to look knowledgeable in your job because the product or service you're dealing with has an 'expert' or scientific image. Pick up here on the icons of the professions who dress entirely in black or white. Black says 'expertise and intellectualism' because it's associated with the church and the law, while white says 'wisdom and compassion' because it's associated with medicine, which is why some cosmetics counters dress their assistants in white

uniforms. To support the non-verbal message being given out, women might need to play down their gender signs so as to appear professionally asexual. Tie hair back off the face and choose small, simple accessories and a natural or unnoticeable make-up.

All these agendas – power, rapport, sexuality, expertise – will almost certainly mix and match in whatever work you do. You will want to appear powerful but approachable, knowledgeable yet friendly. Hence, you'll blend styles in order to create the very best effect. Studies have shown that in business, for example, women who have an extremely masculine or an extremely feminine image are not judged as favourably as those who combine the two, wearing a structured suit but in warm colours, with expert make-up and elegant jewellery and accessories.

CRACKING THE DRESS CODE Overlaying your personal style decisions, you'll also need to take into account the basic unwritten dress code of your company. This is a kind of 'housestyle' that is created by the bosses, who lay down a formal code (no jeans … tie your hair back …), that is then refined by employees who adapt it informally to suit themselves (we all wear black here …). Learn the code and follow it, unless you want to give the non-verbal message to your bosses that you don't care, and to your colleagues that you're not part of the team.

The formal code will be easy to follow. If the office manager or personnel department don't know about it, it doesn't exist – so ask. But there are no written guidelines to an informal dress code – you'll have to work it out for yourself. It will vary not only within professions but also according to which company you work for, which department you work in, which age band you belong to, and what level of seniority you hold. And it may be just as threatening to your colleagues if you dress above your level as it will be to the management if you dress too casually for work. One very obvious example is that there are some jobs where the dress code is still to wear a business suit all the time, such as training or middle management. But conversely there are some, like fashion journalism or PR, where you need to dress 'now' or you are doomed.

The secret of following the unwritten dress code is to check out the following rigorously for your department and your level. What type of clothes do people wear? How formal or casual are they, how fashionable, and in what colours? How many new outfits do people wear over time, and is it acceptable to wear the same thing two days running? What kind of shoes are worn? How much jewellery, and how expensive and outrageous is it? What hairstyles do people generally choose, how long is their hair worn, and is it coloured? What make-up, if any, is worn? As part of your effort to succeed in any new job, make a mental note for the first few days of all these details, until you begin to understand the secret code – and only then go out and start restocking your wardrobe.

FEELING GOOD AT WORK It's important to be in a good emotional state while you are at work. If your body language signals 'moody', then colleagues will start thinking of you as that sort of person. And 'that sort of person' may well find her- or himself being passed over for promotion.

Some recent research from sports psychology suggests that there is a short-term solution to this problem, and that you can use non-verbal techniques to change your mood. Using these techniques will make your body language change spontaneously and genuinely; for a while, at any rate, you will neither feel in a bad mood nor show it non-verbally.

Have you ever sensed your confidence slipping, before that big meeting or during that crucial presentation? Signs of non-confidence are simply a way of silently signalling to others that you feel you can't cope with a situation. Before words were first spoken, human beings called for help by using panic signs. Now we use a toned-down version of those same signs: shaky gestures, a trembling voice, speech stutters, a dry mouth, a pale colour, and bad co-ordination. If your lack of confidence is not well-founded – if you know your stuff but just lack self-belief – then you should try the following strategy.

Start by remembering an occasion when you were confident, when you knew you could do something well and you did do it well. Imagine yourself at that time, seeing what you saw, hearing what you heard, sensing what you sensed. This mental exercise acts as a kind of physiological pump primer, reminding your body of how it feels to be confident. And as you start to remember fully, you'll probably sense yourself responding, relaxing, starting to breathe steadily, and beginning to focus.

As you get in touch with this feeling, exaggerate it just a little. Stand as firmly as you can, maybe with feet slightly apart to steady you. Hold your head high, maybe even tilted back slightly. Breathe deeply and relax even more as you do so. Be aware of your heart rate slowing, imagine your adrenaline dying down, and feel your mouth becoming moist again. You may want

▲ The same task, two different reactions. On the right Mark's obvious confidence in what he's doing is shown by his relaxed movements, gaze towards the task and lack of body tension. Tom both stands back and looks away, trying to disguise a nervousness that is shown by his frown and tense position.

to bite your tongue to encourage saliva; relax your vocal chords to give your voice a lower and more confident quality; say something out loud or count from one to ten just to get rid of any remaining vocal squeaks or trembles.

You'll need to practise feeling confident in this way in order to train your body into responding confidently when you need it to. Once you know you can summon up the state consciously, then give yourself an aide-memoire by adding to your routine a small movement, such as a deep in-breath or 'stand up straight' action. Then, when you're not confident and need to be so, use that same movement to trigger the confident mood and fully remind yourself of the body language you need to adopt.

One warning, though. This 'reminder' is only useful when you're actually skilled but, just for a moment, you've forgotten that fact. Don't force yourself to use confident body language when, in reality, you ought to be nervous – when you're underprepared for a project, for example, or just

▼ **When really motivated, we lean forward intently, use broad gestures, show the classic 'wide-eyed' look that means we are interested and want to know more. When demotivated, we try to pull back, draw our gestures in towards our body, twist our head to one side, let our eyes glaze over or screw them up, frown, and use comfort gestures.**

not skilled enough to cope with the situation. If you really can't perform and you know it, your only solution is to improve. Ask your body to come up with the goods in this situation, and it will simply and quite justifiably refuse.

INCREASING MOTIVATION Whereas the body language of confidence is all about being relaxed and stable, the body language of motivation is about being alert and energetic. Of course, continuous demotivation at work is the type of situation that requires career counselling, not body language. But if you need to get to the end of a boring training course, or plough through the last half-hour of a tedious meeting, then you can persuade your body to provide you with vitality, in much the same way as you persuaded it to provide you with confidence.

You know when you're motivated. Your adrenaline is running high and you're energetic. People see you looking attentively, listening alertly, your whole posture upright, steady and concentrated, your movements quick and certain. So if you find yourself doing just the opposite – leaning back, slumping, hiding a yawn, de-focusing – then you need to get moving and get your energy going. (It's no coincidence that Japanese firms often build in physical exercise for staff as an essential part of their working day.)

Begin by making an excuse to leave the room, pleading a need for the toilet if necessary; once alone, start moving around. It may look foolish kicking off your shoes and jumping up and down in your business suit, but you'll look a whole lot more foolish losing the contract. The aim is to keep going, maybe not until you're sweating profusely, but certainly until you've noticeably raised your heart rate. You can also use the old trick of dabbing icy water on your wrists and the back of your neck to get the blood flowing.

Once back in the meeting or the training course, use the same sort of strategy to achieve the body language of motivation as you did for the body language of confidence. Remember the last time you felt motivated. Reproduce those signals, leaning forward in your seat, drawing your legs back under you as if you are interested, and keeping your breathing quiet but rapid.

If you practise feeling motivated, you can add to your repertoire the ability to be motivated almost on command. And you can develop a trigger of motivated body language similar to your trigger of confident bodytalk – some gesture such as clenching your fist or clicking your fingers that will remind you of your energetic state and allow you to replicate it when you need to.

SURVIVING STRESS You almost certainly know when you feel stressed. Your stomach churns, your breath comes raggedly, your heart pounds. If you feel like this constantly, you need a long-term programme of stress management, which en-courages you to change your whole lifestyle. But if you just occasionally get overwhelmed, then body language techniques can help.

When you feel stressed – perhaps because of some sudden trigger such as bad news about a project, or perhaps because of tension built up during the day – then start by going somewhere where there are no interruptions. This may mean closing your office door firmly and taking the phone off the hook. Sit comfortably, or even lie down on the floor if you can and, just for five minutes, let go completely.

You may find it helps either to think of a time when you were relaxed, or to fantasize about somewhere where you could relax: an island in the sun, a country walk, a warm bath. Allow your whole body to unwind; if it helps, concentrate on each part separately, from your feet up through your legs to your pelvis, stomach and upper chest, across your shoulders down to your arms and hands, and back up to your neck and head. Breathe deeply all the while, counting slowly from one to ten as you do so.

Then lie quietly for just a few minutes, concentrating on your breathing before counting backwards from ten to one and slowly coming back to the here-and-now. Adopt this relaxation sequence as part of your daily routine where you can, but also, fix it in your mind as a memo to your body. Given sufficient practise, simply counting from one to ten slowly will trigger your body into relaxing at times when you haven't got the opportunity to carry out the whole sequence.

The three techniques in this section won't give you deep personal change or solve all your problems. But if you want to finish the project without losing heart, get through the meeting without falling asleep, or make it to the end of the day without screaming, then these body language 'fixes' will do the trick.

▲ When the phone call has gone well, Ben's posture is more upright, balanced and stable; he doesn't need the support of hand to head. His relaxed expression and slight smile signal his good mood, and his more focused gaze indicates that his mind is on the task.

◀ Ben's stressed reaction shows in his slumped, unbalanced posture and tense shoulders. His right hand supports his head in a typical comfort gesture; his left hand slams the phone down – we often let our tension out on objects rather than direct it at people. His slightly defocused gaze shows that he's imagining something – while his expression suggests that whatever he is imagining is none too pleasant.

Coping with colleagues

What makes work situations so challenging is the fact that, with people thrown together day after day in close proximity, office politics develop: alliances, hostilities, power-plays. You need to understand these in order to be able to handle them – but because they'll rarely get talked about without bias, your only real source of insight may be the body language around you.

Start by analyzing the existing pecking order. We're not talking here about formal systems of manager and staff, but about informal hierarchies between you and your colleagues, the clearly defined order of importance in which everyone has their place. What dictates this will depend entirely on what's valued within your particular group: seniority or rank, a higher salary, being married, being talented, being fashionable – or even being male.

To discover just where you are in your group pecking order, observe. The higher in the order you are, the more people will listen to you. If you say something, others lower in the pecking order will pay attention, though people higher than you will feel able to interrupt. The higher you are, the more people will agree with you, nod when you're talking, take up on your suggestions. Men, incidentally, often interrupt in a 'high pecking order' way, whether they are formally your superior or not. If a male colleague does this persistently, a woman needs to fight back, or the non-verbal impression she'll give will be that she accepts her 'low pecking order' role.

⬆ Far left, Rachel seems to want to attract the attention of table-leaning Paul; but he's chatting – in a purely friendly way – to Suzy. In the foreground, Martin's non-verbal pointers are all to Rachel. And what is it that Daniel isn't saying – with his hand to his mouth?

⬆ Two social pairs, Rachel and Martin, Paul and Daniel, block off other people from their interactions by gaze and position. Far left, Fiona's tense shoulders and over-controlled legs and arms signal that she isn't yet relaxed in the others' company; maybe she's a newcomer.

WHOSE SIDE ARE YOU ON? As well as a pecking order, watch out for alliances and hostilities. Simple friendship will be very clear; spot the classic signs not only of people spending time together, but of their being happy to face each other, to have lengthy eye contact, and to 'match' and 'mirror'. When friendship spreads throughout a whole team or department, look for group tie signs such as a tendency to wear the same kind of clothes and go to the same places for a drink after work, and also territorial signs, such as always commandeering the same table in the canteen.

If you want to be part of an alliance, then follow the guidelines that are laid down on pages 35–6 for making friends. The fact that you're working in close proximity will help to reduce considerably the initiation time; the deep-level body matching that you develop while doing the same kind of job often means that you fall into natural harmony. You can also enhance this process by using the guidelines that are given in the sections of this book on rapport, reading minds and understanding personality (from pages 22, 28 and 31). However, bear in mind that work alliances, built up day after day, year after year, are more territorial and defensive than even the most permanent friendship groups (see page 39). So be prepared to sit quietly during the tea break

▼ By now, Fiona is much more at ease in her work situation. But Martin's intrusive posture is making her 'block' him off; she's far more interested in Daniel. Behind, tense positions and expressions show a possible disagreement between Rachel and Suzy. To the right, Paul's blocking arm and bowed head show that he is obviously engrossed in his work.

for quite a while, to laugh along with the jokes for quite a while, and to go to the favourite wine bar after work for quite a while before you're accepted as one of the crowd.

If you aren't accepted by colleagues at your place of work – through jealousy, perhaps, competition or simply because you don't fit in for some reason or the other – that may be difficult to spot because it's not acceptable to be openly hostile in a situation where you have to work together every day. If things are inexplicably going badly for you, then look out for what are called 'leakages', where a pleasant expression is suddenly interrupted by a microcue of a more negative emotion.

Men will show leakages of anger more than women, who typically show warmth or regret more easily. So, if you are successful on a project, and you turn to find someone else's congratulatory smile fleetingly marred by a mouth movement of the sort that can only be called bitter, what you're seeing is jealousy. If your performance is being compared with someone else's, and that person's face momentarily becomes tense and aggressive, what you're watching is competition. If you tell a joke and among the laughter you spot the occasional mocking eye raised to skywards toward heaven, then what you're seeing is hostility. Forewarned is definitely forearmed.

If you do see any of these things, then having to work with those people will be difficult, so you'll really have to change things. If it's a group that is against you, don't try to tackle them together; they'll take their non-verbal lead from each other and close ranks. Instead, divide and conquer; if you face an adversary on her (or his) own, she (or he) will be much easier to deal with. Discussing a project together on a one-to-one basis, you can use all your rapport skills to make your two sets of body language fit until you're matching and turn-taking easily. If you do this,

then the silent message will be neither 'I'm against you ...' nor 'You're getting to me ...'; rather it will be 'We're similar and I want us to get on well together'. Without really knowing why, your adversary will unconsciously feel slightly better about you. And, equally unconsciously, as you match her or him more, you will start to feel more sympathetic towards that person. Because of basic physiology and life conditioning, you will find it more difficult to match male colleagues than female ones. However, if you use this approach consistently and with everyone with whom you have disagreements, you will gradually, over time, notice that they feel less antagonistic towards you, and that you feel more friendly towards them.

LOVE AT WORK Finally, what about sex in the office? You can tell who's attracted to whom by watching their display behaviours (see page 57) – though you won't get exactly the same signals in the office as you would in social situations. It will all be toned down because of the context, and the woman in particular won't be nearly as obvious in her flirting signs because she knows that people are watching her. When courtship turns into a relationship, though, the positions are often reversed. She may feel more secure and will start to let her feelings show; he may be less obvious now that he has attained his goal. So you can often tell that sex is now on the agenda when she starts looking at him, and he stops looking at her. This is particularly true if he's married and is having an affair, while if both of them are married then overnight they may both start ignoring each other totally.

If it's you yourself who are having an office romance and want to hide it, then you must keep your body language friendly rather than suddenly either passionate or hostile – both of which are instant giveaways. Instead, remember how you used to relate before you became involved and

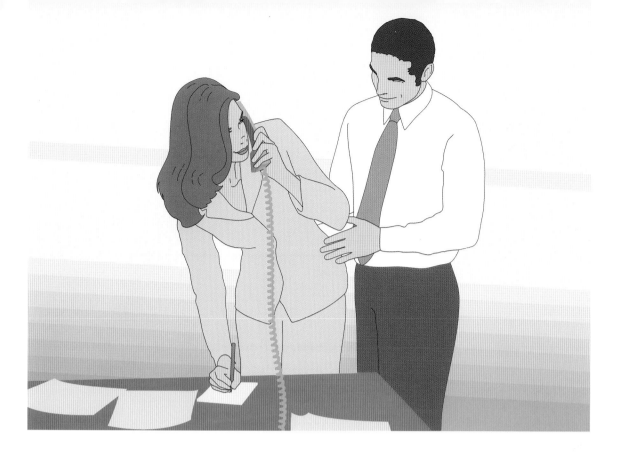

▲ ▶ No one should be sexually harassed, not least at work. But if it does happen, then it's less effective – and less likely to discourage further advances – to shrink away and smile placatingly, as Heather is doing here in the illustration above. More likely to deter the culprit is to face him directly and stare directly at him unsmilingly, while verbally making it clear that you don't want any further advances, just as the illustration on the right shows Heather doing.

behave just like that. Make sure that your body language signals 'friendly colleague' rather than 'passionate lover'. Check the distance you stand from each other: friends are comfortable at between 5 and 1.2 m (18 and 4 ft) apart, lovers are happy to move closer – while secret lovers sit on opposite sides of the room. Monitor the amount of eye contact you have; friends are happy to look away, lovers gaze, secret lovers never even glance. Be aware of the voice tone you take with each other: friends keep a normal voice tone, lovers let their tone drop and slow down, secret lovers hardly speak at all.

Handling your boss

Whether you work directly for a boss or simply report to one, you need to handle her, or him, effectively. Start by identifying, broadly, what style of leadership she, or he, follows so that you can react appropriately. Three commonly recognized styles are 'autocratic', 'democratic' and 'laissez-faire'. A boss can major in one or have elements of all three, and each style can carry with it a particular body language approach. If your body language complements your boss's leadership style, then you will have a problem-free relationship. If your non-verbal approach contradicts hers, then you may have problems.

The autocratic boss – who is traditionally likely to be a man – values the non-verbal signs of status that come with the job – the desk, the nameplate, the company car. So he may reinforce that status with his body language, dressing expensively and formally. He'll probably use a classic 'leader's' posture, with straight back, squared shoulders, controlled movements, head held high. He will keep barriers between you, closing his door,

▲ A democratic boss's finger point is unthreatening because of his other body language: bent head, informal manner, and the fact that he allows his employee to sit next to him and on the same side of the desk. It has a different impact than the finger point, opposite.

sitting behind his desk, making sure by his expressionless face and unemotional voice that you don't get too friendly. He'll stare you down if you begin to get out of line, and will let his displeasure show in his expression and tone. Women who play the autocratic boss can be criticized as 'inhuman'.

If you want to be the perfect employee, never try to undermine that formal body language. Treat him formally, knocking when you enter, waiting to be told to sit down, not moving to his side of the desk without permission. Wait for his turn-taking signals, and don't interrupt him. Smile and be pleasant, but don't laugh or chat more than he does or he'll see you as a time-waster. And, if your autocratic boss is a woman, never, ever try to outdress her.

▲ An autocratic boss uses a directive head tilt, eye control and finger point, emphasized by her use of the pen. Her employee stands to show respect, but offsets height advantage by keeping her distance, bowing her head slightly, bending her knee and smiling.

▼ The laissez-faire boss's pointing finger keeps his employee at a distance, and his pulled-back body and averted head adds to the effect. His employee takes care not to 'threaten' him by standing well back and up and not demanding eye contact.

Very different is the 'democratic' leader, traditionally more likely to be female. What's important to her is the people side of the job, so she'll use body language to build personal relationships. She'll arrange her office for maximum access, with a chair near hers, or an informal 'social' area for meetings. She'll usually adopt sociable body language, with a positive expression and clear signals of rapport; she'll tell you something rather than write it down, and will be happy to pop into your office rather than make you come to hers. She'll often touch you, as a gesture of support or congratulation. Men, by the way, who adopt democratic leader body language can be misinterpreted as being over-friendly.

To succeed with this type of boss, you need to tread a careful line. Go with her open-door policy,

whether you're at ease with it or not, and match her rapport with friendly non-verbal signals of your own – relaxed movements, smiling and voice tone. But don't think that she wants you to act as a peer and start interrupting or talking over her; rather, aim for 'modified rapport', where you act in a friendly manner, but still always wait for her lead in speaking or acting.

The laissez-faire boss keeps clear, letting you do your job in your way. More men are likely to adopt this approach. This type of boss may be an introvert (see page 33) who has got promotion through talent rather than through people skills. So he may set up barriers – to keep his stimulation levels down – while not being in the least status-conscious. And he may be quite friendly, but lack expression and eye contact because he doesn't want to get involved. He keeps his distance, often being away from the office, communicating through memos, or hardly checking on you at all.

Here, your body language needs to emphasize self-sufficiency. Act in a more equal way, matching him and holding eye contact in a way that reassures him that you can cope. Show the non-verbal signs of motivation (see pages 87–8), so that he knows you will get the job done. But don't expect high levels of interaction; keep meetings short, sit at an angle from him so he doesn't feel invaded, expect him to look away or appear distracted. Expect to be left alone for long periods – and when he does reappear, give him a report that shows by your body language that you're independent, confident and effective.

READING THE SIGNS Having established your boss's general patterns of behaviour, it's a good idea to analyze much more specifically what his or her body language signs mean in particular situations.

Perhaps the most basic thing you'll want to know is whether your boss is in a bad mood. As it often isn't acceptable to show this at work, he or she may not tell you, but it will show in other

▲ She's raised her head and straightened up, but not far enough to constitute a welcome. Her gaze is defocused, showing she's still thinking about something else. It may be better to come back later.

ways. Look for signs of stress and tension – kept in by tight shoulders and pinched lips, an expressionless face and a heaviness of movement; or let out by a raised voice, sharp syllables and a tendency to treat objects violently, slamming down phones with a click or closing doors with a bang.

Also learn the signs of whether your boss is busy or approachable. A closed door is the formal sign, but even if it's open, he or she may be using subtle 'leave me alone' signals, such as a shoulder or arm blocking your approach from the door, raised shoulders to cut out noise, a head bowed over the desk. Interestingly, the opposite signals – a lean back in the chair, a stare out of the window, a defocused, opaque gaze, and, for a man, feet on the desk – don't necessarily mean that it's OK for you to interrupt. These may be signs of being in downtime (see pages 44–5). In this case, your boss may actually not be nearly as interruptible as when seemingly making notes, but is in fact alert

▲ Her tense back and hands betray negative feelings and her mouth pushes forward in an angry pout, even though her direct gaze encourages interaction. Is it you who has irritated her or someone else?

▲ Her smile is welcoming, her tilted head indicates interest and a willingness to listen. She may be busy, but her bodytalk is entirely welcoming. This could be the right day to ask for a raise.

to what is happening outside, eyes scanning the room, ears 'pricked' to overhear conversations.

Next, learn the signals your boss uses to guide interactions with you. They'll be subtly different from those of conversation, because you both have a job to do, and because your boss is in charge and you are following instructions. He or she may direct the conversation, with a deliberate pause and head movement requiring an answer from you, a look and raised eyebrows to check if you have understood something. A circling hand gesture may mean it's time to move on to another point, while eye contact and a nod may mean that an instruction has been completed. At the end of an interaction, when your boss wants to be alone, he or she may shuffle papers, shift in his or her chair, or tap both hands on the arms as if to get up and get on. At this point, a male boss will tend to be more direct, looking at his watch or getting up from his chair to indicate the end of the meeting.

Finally it's useful to know, even a few seconds in advance, if a boss going to say yes or no to something. Here, micro-movements come into their own; typically, as someone considers a proposal they indicate with these subtle shifts just what their reaction is. Watch carefully, and you'll see the micro-nod for yes – or the even more subtle blink that reflects the head nod and also marks key phrases with which someone agrees. Conversely, notice the micro-shake for no, or a parallel negating movement of a finger. If your boss is still undecided about something, he or she may give an 'unsure' signal, most obviously an up-and-down shift of the shoulders, a 'balancing' movement of the hands, or a wiggle of the lips.

Of course, each boss will have her or his own special set of non-verbal codes. So you'll need to check out not only all the above body language sequences but also any others that are key for your boss, then tailor your response to them.

Tactics for meetings

Despite the fact that a business meeting is officially about discussion, it's the underlying body language that makes or breaks it. So look at where you'll hold the meeting. What's your aim? A boardroom may well have large tables and status icons that will make the meeting formal and business-like, but holding it in any kind of social area with a sofa and coffee table will help build good relationships. If you allow people into a private office environment, the fact that it is on your territory will put you more in control, while using a neutral meeting room may make it easier to create co-operative teamwork.

Next, look at seating. For conversation and group-building, a table where everyone can sit in a circle or side by side is best. For cohesion, choose a smaller table that will make participants feel closer in both senses of the term; for creativity, allow space to spread out. If there's likely to be a competitive edge and you want to increase it,

▲ Charlotte and Justin (left) arrive for a meeting with Yvonne and Frank. The first signs are good, with friendly smiles and formal handshakes. But Justin shows his tension by his slightly false smile, and Yvonne's 'hands behind back' hints that she may feel isolated.

place people on opposite sides of the table; if you want to reduce it, place them on the same side. Put whoever is controlling the meeting at the head or at the middle of the long side of a crowded table; if there's an individual you want to keep under control, put them alone on the long side of the table, opposite more than one person.

Also look at how you're going to welcome people as they arrive. There are subtle non-verbal messages in every method of welcome. Meeting participants at the lift and escorting them to the meeting room makes some feel respected, while to allow a friendly, long-standing client to come up unescorted might give him or her the message, 'You're one of us'. Keeping participants waiting in

▲ Tension is building. Frank is biding his time. Yvonne and Justin show their anxiety in posture and expression, though Yvonne, as many women do, hides her worry with a false smile. Justin's frown shows serious concern. Charlotte is the only one with open, inclusive gestures – if she's to rescue the meeting she needs to move quickly.

▲ Now there is open disagreement. Charlotte and Frank are 'fencing' with their pens, a very typical aggressive gesture in business. Charlotte still shows her willingness to listen by her head tilt and slight smile. But she'll get no help from Mark, who has withdrawn, with protective gesture and blank expression – as has Yvonne.

the foyer until the exact time of the meeting can give the impression that you're busy and important, while inviting them up beforehand for a pre-meeting coffee may imply they're friends.

Remember all that's been said about greeting techniques (from page 19), letting your strategy tend towards the formal as being more suitable for the work context – a handshake, for example, is seen in the business context as showing your efficiency and competence. But also be flexible – greetings vary according to four factors: the culture of the company, your status compared with that of the person you're greeting, the length of time you've known them, and how long since you last saw them. In some professions, you lose kudos for not kissing the most tenuous of contacts on both cheeks; in others, such behaviour even with long-term colleagues is out of place.

HIDDEN AGENDA Whatever's on the formal agenda, watch closely for the participants' real motives. The American psychologist David McClelland has identified three types of business objective:

'affiliation', an agenda for group cohesion and good feeling; 'achievement', an agenda about getting the task done; 'power' an agenda of being in control. Each has its own specific body language pattern.

An affiliator – typically a woman or a sociable man – will probably arrive early to greet people and talk to them. She will want to contact everyone, and may actually cause a delay in the meeting, as she is so busy 'touching down'. She'll typically sit where she can see everyone and make sure they're included, and her body language will reflect this, with lots of eye contact, smiles and turn-giving. She'll show signs of tension if there's conflict, and will use a calming voice and hand movements to appease people and reconcile them. She may stay behind afterwards, chatting.

An achiever will tend to arrive strictly on time; he or she won't want to waste a minute of the day. If he does speak to anyone beforehand, it will usually be someone crucial; he'll often choose to sit next to that person at the table, or alternatively, next to someone who may block the project and needs to be 'persuaded'. At the meeting, this task-orientated person will have the right equipment, notepad and pen, relevant papers. He'll want to keep a strict agenda, will calmly hear everyone out as long as they're speaking relevantly, but will get irritated at what he regards as 'waffle'. He'll relax once key decisions have been made, and may then leave early to go on to another meeting.

Someone who wants power at a meeting – typically a man or high-flying woman – may arrive just slightly late (a typical power-play), to make a point or to get some motion passed, so you have to wait for him. If he does arrive in time to socialize, he'll often spend most time with those who are also in power, such as the chairperson. He'll typically try to sit in the 'power position' – the head or short side of the table – or in the middle of a long side if he wants to influence a large number of people. During the meeting, he'll tend to talk loudly and quickly, and will interrupt if things aren't going his way. He'll stay right to the end, in case something happens when he's not there, but once the influential people have left, he'll leave too.

Most people have one of these basic agenda patterns in most meetings they attend, though they can change agendas on particular occasions. But, equally, many will combine the three patterns, aiming for a little of each. Monitor agendas – in other participants and also in yourself – because they won't always tally with what people say they want from a meeting and you may need to be warned of this in advance. Also, once you've identified what agendas people have, you can then use them all to help you achieve a successful meeting, letting the 'cohesion' participants build up a good group feeling beforehand, then utilizing the 'task' and 'power' participants' reactions during the meeting as your mine detectors for whether things are on course and what power-plays are currently in operation.

TAKING THE CHAIR A meeting is a group conversation so, if you yourself are chairing it, you'll need all your normal conversational skills, but with the added challenge of having to guide the group towards an agreement.

Begin by signalling your leadership at the start. Use your confidence trigger (see pages 85–7) if you need to, then sit tall and straight and look around, holding eye contact with everyone and waiting until they are quiet before starting. Throughout, keep looking at everyone – a message that you're still in charge. Remember that, if you're in a predominantly male environment, emotional openness can be seen as ineffectiveness, so control your facial expression and avoid showing overt anger or distress.

One of your chief tasks will be to show people when they can speak. Watch out for signs that they want to – normal turn-seeking behaviours, yet aimed not at the person who's talking, but at you as chairperson. So as well as keeping one ear on the speaker, you also have to check for intakes of breath, for irritated finger tapping, for those who are trying to get eye contact with you, for those who are signalling 'my turn' with a finger lift or a minute wave of a pen. When you do give a participant permission to speak, clarify this with an emphasized turn-giving wave of the hand in their direction, to show everyone who now has the floor. Give the speaker your attention by turning to them and looking at them, which will encourage others to do the same.

Silencing people may be more of a challenge than getting them to speak. You may have to use the more challenging methods that you use in conversation (see pages 24–8), and if these don't work, say their name (a word most people will respond to, however engrossed they are) along with a frown to indicate that there's a problem. You can also use a 'silence' signal – there are universally acknowledged ones, such as tapping on a glass or with a gavel.

During the meeting, you may also need to guide people towards agreement or defuse conflict when agreement seems far away. So constantly check participants' emotions via their body language. Note those who appear uninvolved, shown by a slight lean back, stretched-out legs, and a hand supporting the head. Re-involve these people by asking them a question or inviting a comment. Also note, from the body matching, where alliances are being formed and broken during the meeting; if someone is changing sides, for example, their body language will signal this in advance as they 'match' or 'mirror' the person they're now allied to even before their words show that they have shifted their opinion.

What if there is trouble? Keep an eye open for 'deceit' signals (see page 72) because once someone starts to lie, very often other participants sense that and start to get irritated or upset. And whether or not anyone is lying, if you hear voices rising and see angry expressions, then even if what is being said seems harmless, take care. It's

▲ As they stand to leave, everyone except Yvonne has the tense, upright stance, raised head and direct gaze that signal 'attack'. Yvonne is retreating, dropping her head and eye contact to signal 'I'm not a threat'.

wise, at this point, to call for silence and allow a cooling-off period while you talk for a few moments, to allow irritation to die away.

At the end of every meeting, make sure that decisions have been agreed non-verbally as well as verbally. Look at each participant in turn and check their agreement signals, watching for eye contact, uncrossed arms, micro-nods of the head or 'it's done' signals such as closing a laptop or folder and pushing away from the table. If instead you get a hostile posture, crossed arms and frowning or unbalanced facial expression, micro-shakes of the head or a shift of the shoulders, you need to go back and rediscuss or reconfirm the item. If you fail to do this, participants may – whatever they say at the time – 'mis-remember' what was discussed, or 'misunderstand' what was agreed.

You and the client

If you deal with the public, in a retail or business setting, you need to adopt a wholly different style of body language from normal.

The non-verbal message in any service situation should be, 'I'm here to help' – so body language needs to be alert and motivated. But the message isn't, 'I'm your friend', so normal social signals often need to be toned down: you may smile but not too widely, approach close but not too closely, give eye contact but not in a challenging way.

At the same time as being helpful, you also have to be in charge. Because you're responsible to the company you work for, you have to use the body language of polite assertiveness, your posture confident, your movements sure, your eye contact direct. Because you'll be meeting the client or customer for only a short time, you have to show them the ropes with larger-than-life gestures to make sure they know what to do quickly and easily.

WHAT KIND OF CLIENT? Above and beyond this general body language, you also need to treat each person slightly differently, depending on

▲ The body language of service – how not to do it. The assistants' animation, shown in gesture and expression, focuses in towards themselves and totally excludes the customer. They should be facing towards the shop floor, enabling a customer to catch their eye, toning down their social involvement with each other so that a customer feels able to approach.

what kind of customer or client they are. The neutral client doesn't actually want to interact on any kind of personal level – she may not even register you as a person. She may look over you or through you as she speaks, give you little facial expression and no rapport signals. You, in return, need to respect her need for a non-relationship. Adopt a neutral tone, and don't try to engage her with eye contact, let alone chat. Sign her off as soon as you can and she'll be happy.

The friendly client wants the exact opposite. She may not want to chat, but she does want to feel that she's relating to you as another human being. She'll usually give you rapport signals as clear as if she were talking to someone she knew well, in a friendly voice, with smiles and open gestures. You can respond in kind, though of course in a toned-down way; it's up to the client to take the lead and for you to follow.

Conversely, a client who is a 'follower' will want you to take charge. This type is most often seen in situations where people are unfamiliar with or nervous of the procedures involved, such as plane flights. She will almost duck as she approaches you, head slightly bobbed and eyes lowered. She may appear timid, with a nervy laugh or wary gestures, and will tend to take up less space than normal. In response, you have to appear calm and in control, and give her directions that are even more emphatic than usual, in a clear voice.

Other clients want to feel in charge, because they're wary of you or because they're wary in case the service you offer goes wrong. The

'dominator' type will immediately stare you down as she approaches, her face frowning, her voice loud and firm. She will often try to encroach on your space to prove her dominance, leaning over the counter, placing her bag or coat on it, or grabbing your arm. A variation on this type is the overtly aggressive client – usually so because she has a specific complaint, and easily spotted by her angry body language. It's tempting to match bad behaviour with bad behaviour, but you mustn't. Instead, keep smiling, and however difficult it may be, try dropping your shoulders and head just

▼ Once rapport is established or re-established, then facing the customer directly with clear eye contact will involve her in the interaction, while matching her head tilt will show a willingness to understand her needs.

slightly as you talk: studies of conflict situations have shown that lowering the body slightly reduces the tension 90 per cent of the time. By giving a client such signals, you're telling her that she's in the right; whether or not she is, she'll be much easier to handle once she's been appeased.

Reaching agreement

There have been many books written about how body language can persuade even the most unwilling client to buy – but in reality, clients spot manipulation and respond best to a genuine desire to meet their needs.

The first step, therefore, is to greet your client with genuine pleasure. In a retail context, catch her eye and smile as she enters (though if she shows the 'just looking, not touching' eye-sweep of the true browser, then don't bother to go up to her). If you are contacting your client on the phone, stand up and smile at the start of the call to give your voice a boost in enthusiasm.

Take time to establish rapport. If you're face-to-face with a client, use all the suggestions given on page 22. On the phone, talk for a while to allow yourself to register the client's voice tone and rhythm. Then match these verbal cues in just the same way as you would match gestures, until you're both feeling at ease with each other.

Next, present the product, be that an actual object or a concept such as a new business idea. The key here is to gauge just what the client needs to know. If she is a looker/toucher (see page 32), give her the product or the promotional material to see or handle. If she is a listener, present the information in words, speaking fluently and confidently: hesitation can suggest you're insincere or incompetent. In both cases use all your rapport skills and add in some 'palm-down' gestures to encourage trust.

Once you've presented the product, back off. You might think that talking is the only way to sell, but actually, most clients need downtime (see from pages 45–6) to think through their decision. Move back, literally or metaphorically, and keep quiet. While they're thinking, watch them carefully. Be aware whether your client is using open body language (for example open arms, open facial expression) or closed (crossed arms and legs, frown, pursed mouth), and whether they're using forward body language (forward lean, forward head tilt) or backward (leaning back, raised chin). Then use the following guidelines in order to judge what to do next.

If the client's body language is both closed and backward leaning, they're feeling uninvolved and bored – you need to spark their interest and get them re-involved with your proposition. If the client's body language is closed but forward leaning, they're feeling threatened and confrontative – so back off from heavy tactics, defuse their anger and let them feel more secure. If the client's body language is open and backward leaning, they're considering your proposition but are not yet convinced – find out what is really needed in order to close the sale. But if the client's body language is both open and forward leaning, then they're yours – you can move forward to close the sale, confident that they'll go with you.

Whatever the outcome, whether your client buys or not, use body language to end well. If their final answer is a genuine no, you'll know it by the client's definite head shake or their firm voice tone as they decides not to take things further. Hide your feelings; a pleasant, undisappointed reaction gives the non-verbal message that their decision has been respected, and leaves them feeling good about any further approach on another occasion. If the answer is yes, however, you can show your delight, with a smile, a nod, a rise in voice volume and pitch. Your aim is to give the message, 'You made the right decision', which will reward the client, let them feel good, and make them want to deal with you again.

Interview success

The initial step when you know you have an interview is usually to find out more about your prospective new employer to inform your performance. But don't just gather details from what they say in the brochure or on the phone. Go one step further: look at their non-verbal communication and interpret that, too.

◀ Already Tina has cause for worry; her very formal business suit is just slightly at odds with the seemingly more relaxed ethos of the firm. But she could be helping herself more than she is – with a more obviously energetic posture, direct eye contact and friendly smile that matches Lesley's welcoming expression.

▼ Again, though Lesley is encouraging her with body and head tilt, Tina is throwing the job away minute by minute. Probably due to nervousness, she's slumped, with a downcast gaze and sulky mouth. The message she's giving is that she's not interested in the job.

▲ New interviewee Sarah is not only making a better impression, but is also allowing Lesley to be more relaxed and therefore more receptive. Lesley's responding smile and head tilt suggests that she is impressed by Sarah.

Start by looking at their advertisement and the application pack they send – not the words, but the statement made by the body language aspects. Is this a firm with a glossy application pack? This may mean they are doing well, or it may mean that they want to have (rather than actually having) status and wealth. Does their badly photocopied application form mean that they don't pay much attention to presentation, or that the post they want to fill isn't important?

How many pictures of the company chairperson do you see in their brochure as opposed to shots of the working team (or of men rather than women, product rather than people, company headquarters rather than product). What do these signals tell you about their business approach? If you can, visit the workplace and look at the staff – for example, as they leave for their lunch break. Check all you see against the environment and appearance to learn about a company.

Let everything you've learned inform your preparation for the interview, not only in what you plan to say but also in your body language. For example, many people simply wear their 'business suit' to interviews – which is fine if it is a 'suit' company. If it's a company where suits are regarded as boring, you may do better wearing something more creative. Your outfit still needs to be more upmarket than you would normally wear: the non-verbal statement you should be making is that this interview is important to you. But you can customize your clothes (and make-up and hairstyle) quite specifically to the company if you have correctly read the signs.

Equally, let your general body language also signal your fit with the company ethos. If it's formal or hierarchical, let your posture and expression match this. If it's more informal and co-operative, allow your body language to be more relaxed, though never casual; you have to be seen to be on your best behaviour. Signal throughout, to everyone you meet, 'I'll fit in to this company'.

INTERVIEW BODY LANGUAGE Before the interview itself, read the sections of this book on how to adopt the body language sequences of relaxation, confidence and motivation (see pages 85–8). They can help by letting you feel genuinely calm during the preliminaries, but then be alert and self-assured as you go into the interview room.

Once there, don't be put off by the room format. Some interviewers deliberately put a candidate at a disadvantage by placing them in a slightly lower than normal chair, or creating a formal barrier with a desk that non-verbally reinforces your 'subordinate' status. Ignore this: every candidate will be in the same position. Sit straight on your chair – any leg crossing or sideways lean can make your posture appear awkward.

It's crucial to be relaxed so keep your hands together in your lap to start with – otherwise you might be tempted to fidget, a standard sign of nervousness. Don't completely stop yourself from making gestures, though, as this will slow down your fluency rate and your verbal clarity. If you're anxious, pause just slightly before you answer any question – thus giving you time to think, but also allowing you to appear seriously thoughtful.

▲ Has Tina got the job? Probably not: Lesley's smile does not reach her eyes, she's turning away from Tina – and is pulling back slightly from the handshake.

If you don't understand something, or when you come to ask questions of the interviewer rather than being asked, then adopt the non-threatening 'query' expression (head on one side, slight frown, half-smile). This not only signals that you want to know more, but also reassures the speaker that your need to know is not a reflection of her (or his) failure to express herself.

A final key to success, curiously enough, is to give your interviewer signals that you approve of him or her. We tend to think of interviewers as being in such positions of authority that they

◀ Has Sarah got the job? Very probably: Lesley's smile is genuine and involves all her facial muscles, she's turned directly towards Sarah, and she's leaning in to the handshake as if she wants it to continue. Sarah is at the very least in with a chance.

the interaction? Do they respond to your answers with slight headshakes? Are they steadily diminishing their amount of facial expression, in case they show what they really feel? Or are they, for the same reasons, showing just too much approval, giving false smiles and a surfeit of nods to compensate for the rejection they know they're about to hand you?

If you do spot these negative signs before the end of an interview, then you can act, though it takes courage. Change your body language – in any way you can. Talk less, talk more. Smile less, smile more. Use your hands more – or less. Many of these body language strategies may seem like interview suicide. But if you're convinced that you've already failed, then you've nothing to lose by experimenting with them.

Conversely, you will know you're doing well if the interviewer is interested in what you have to say – shown by a forward lean or an open body posture. A longer interview than given to other candidates can be a positive non-verbal statement of interest – though don't interpret a shorter one pessimistically if it's accompanied by genuine approval signals. A heated exchange can be good news if accompanied by enthusiastic gestures and an excited facial expression. Above all, however, look for signs of reciprocal acceptance – matching smiles, eye contact, head nods.

If you see these signs, you can't guarantee success. There may be other suitable candidates whose formal qualifications are better than yours. But if you don't get the post, you can at least reassure yourself; you know that the interviewer unconsciously thought you were good enough even if the end result didn't reflect this.

don't need approval. But studies have shown three consistent body language signals being positively correlated with interview success: smiling, nodding and keeping friendly eye contact. Of course, none of these body language elements may have anything to do with a candidate's real ability to do the job; rather, they're non-verbal signals of acceptance from interviewee to interviewer.

DID YOU GET IT? The main clues as to whether you've succeeded at an interview will probably not be obvious as you leave. To tell how you're doing, you need to check the signs during the interview.

Is the interviewer searching for questions to ask you, signalled by their frequently looking up or to the left with a slight frown? Are they leaning well back from the desk, literally withdrawing from

Leading your team

You've changed jobs to a new one with higher status. As time passes and you grow into your new responsibilities, you'll start to display the body language of leadership – all the signals of being top of the pecking order (see page 89), but magnified and formalized.

Your posture may become slightly more erect, spontaneously increasing your height and breadth – both non-verbal signs of dominance in ape

▲ Preparing a project: postures are static, attentive, ready to learn. People may be unsure of what's going to happen, as shown by the clear distance between them and their protective arm positions, but their head angles show that they are attentive and motivated.

groups, where the bigger and stronger the animal, the more likely it is to be a leader. You may take on the particular expression known as a 'plus' face, with head up, a direct gaze and a serious facial expression. You'll be more likely to take first turn, to claim more space, to touch subordinates and to act in a friendly way to superiors.

Despite what many books claim, you can't become a leader just by starting to do all these things. Simply adopting a type of body language can work temporarily, but can't long-term unless it signals a genuine change in attitude. In particular, if you're being promoted within the company, where everyone will be able to compare your new signals to the way you behaved before the promotion, the new you will be noted with scepticism.

What you can do is to make sure that, as you develop leadership skills, your body language isn't undermining them, and that you aren't still acting like a follower. So check your body language regularly against the above-mentioned signals. If, a few months into your promotion, you're still finding it difficult to speak readily, to go first or to act confidently, these are signs that you aren't growing into your new role.

A word of warning here, for women. As part of their way of coping in life, women typically develop positive social skills. In particular, they smile and nod. But if overused, this kind of body language can indicate submission or placation, thus undermining a woman's authority, particularly if there are men in the team. So, when first moving into a leadership position, it may be useful for you, as a woman, to tone down and de-emphasize these signs, smiling rarely or nodding only when something really meets with your approval. It may seem hard-hearted, but it may also mean that you're taken a great deal more seriously.

MOTIVATING THE TROOPS One of the key skills of leadership is encouraging your staff to do a good job – and discouraging them from doing a bad one. You need to learn not only to tell your staff when they are doing well or badly, but to back up those messages with your body language; studies have proved that mixing positive words and negative non-verbal communication confuses and angers, while mixing negative words and positive non-verbal communication makes people think you're weak and can be easily manipulated.

Praise or encouragement, then, needs to be accompanied by genuine signs of approval: a smile, a nod, an enthusiastic voice tone. If you are a natural toucher and so is your team member, then you can add occasional contact on shoulder or back, anonymous parts of the body that have no sexual ambiguity. Because touch reaches the nerve centres more quickly and effectively than either sight or sound, this will make the praise more meaningful and more motivating.

When it comes to reprimanding employees, genuinely angry body language is almost never a good idea. First, it makes hackles rise and can create long-term resentment. Second, if you're really angry, your agitated body state will override any ability to communicate coherently and effectively. In general then, if you feel that unmistakable surge of energy that accompanies anger, take time out to turn away for a moment, take a few deep breaths and calm your body down. After that, an expressionless face will carry the clear message that you're displeased, as will a low voice with emphasis only on the critical words.

Just occasionally, however, a short, sharp burst of irritation can work wonders – particularly if you're someone who is usually even-tempered and supportive. Letting your voice rise and harden just slightly, letting a frown appear and your gestures become faster and sharper can give an recalcitrant employee a hint of what your future displeasure might mean.

Project body language

Any project, of any length – from a two-year fund-raising drive down to a Monday-morning meeting – passes through a number of stages, each recognizable by its own characteristic body language. If you are aware of these signals, you

can tell how each project is going, and what non-verbal interventions you need to make.

The first stage is preparation. This doesn't just mean planning and preparing, but also achieving a good group feeling and making sure that everyone is happy and committed. The group may well be moving to a slow rhythm as members gradually gear up to the task; there will be lots of coffee-making, sitting, thinking and talking. Even with a group that has known each other for years, it should be obvious from the team's increasingly matching body language that rapport is growing in preparation for the new project.

As leader, move around and interact quietly with group members, using your non-verbal skills

▲ Energizing: movement becomes more marked, showing that group members are starting to act and react. People move closer, match posture and gesture; it's much more likely that they will smile and laugh – or take on irritated expressions and let their voices rise. Papers will be spread more untidily, while handwriting may well become larger and less readable.

to help them make contact with each other. You can also encourage group identification through matching; in most business groups, you won't be able to do this formally, though in groups such as theatre companies or sports teams, you can get people to sing, dance, exercise or bathe together. You will know that things are working when you

see individuals' body language starting to synchronize; if you don't, let preparation run for a little longer, encouraging the group to talk and share activities more fully. Don't push people on, try to get them moving too early or cut this stage short; people need time to get into synchrony.

The next, energizing stage is about action. People will be feeling more lively. Their movement speed will increase – and, as it increases, they'll get yet more energy. Voices will rise in pitch, volume and pace and, as problems arise, you may hear those same voices become irritated or angry. But the work will get done. At this point, you yourself should be energizing people. Let your voice rise and others' voices will follow; let

▲ As the project moves towards its goal, the group's body language reaches a peak of energy and cohesion. The whole group may match and move in synchrony, focusing on one thing. At the moment when the job is done, there may be a spontaneous outburst of noise, applause, laughter, as the group celebrates and body tension is released.

your actions become more energetic and others' will be, too. Urge people on in a firm, clear voice. And don't worry about disagreements – they're a natural part of the process. What you need to do is keep people's energy up – and if it starts to flag, to get them moving around. If all goes well, keep clear and don't interfere.

There'll come a point where you've reached your goal – be that the target reached in your fund-raising drive or the final decision made in your meeting. Then every team needs wind-down time, however brief. Here, they celebrate what they've done, start tidying up, and reflect on what's happened. People will at first feel high, want to relax and let their hair down – you'll observe rising voices and freer movement. After that, they'll be quiet and reflective, sitting around alone, simply thinking, or with one or two others, chatting. For a brief project, expect an extra cup of coffee and just a few minutes of note-taking; for a large project, be prepared for a roaring night out and several weeks of filing.

▲ **Relaxing: people will tend to chat in pairs, with lots of individual eye contact and smiles. They will also typically lean back or slump, and their gestures will be far less formal. This bodytalk signals relaxation – but also a preparation for leaving the group.**

At this point, when the end is in sight, make sure people do have a chance to celebrate, even if only briefly over lunch. Congratulate your team and then let go, no longer urging them on but allowing them time to wind-down. Let your non-verbal approach show that you're pleased and proud, and that they deserve time to relax. Only then begin again, preparing and energizing your team, as you start the ball rolling once more.

5 reading the clues

While all body language is fascinating, it's a good idea to be alerted to particular signals that are important to note. This chapter highlights key body areas and, within these, some vital signs with some of the many different interpretations you can make of each one.

A picture dictionary of body language

It used to be thought that any single body language signal meant only one thing, but the most recent research makes it clear that a non-verbal signal can mean any number of things, depending on the context. To understand this, you need first to check a person's whole body language – appearance, posture, gesture, expression, eye movement, touch patterns and physical functions. Then you need to check a person's background, their culture and upbringing to see if this affects the way they present themselves. Does their body language show any 'personalization', signs that the person has adopted general signals to suit their own personality. Finally, check out the situation in which you see any particular body language sign, to confirm the context in which it is happening: other people's responses and events before and after.

▼ Uneven shoulders and torso

The level of a person's shoulders is even and balanced almost all the time. When the level is noticeably different and shoulders are tilted unevenly, then that's often a body language signal of some kind of imbalance in what a person is thinking. It's a residual sign of the signal humans use when startled, and it shows they're trying to make a decision or consider the options: a shifting movement of the hands and arms, as if quite literally 'weighing' the alternatives.

Shoulder imbalance is a toned-down, subtle version of this weighing movement. A person's shoulder level will alternate, first one shoulder

then the other going up and down, or the person will give a slight wriggle, as if to shake off something across their upper back. Their head, too, may tilt, in synchrony. These movements may accompany a person's own words about which decision to make – or may be performed less obviously as they react to the possibilities being outlined by someone else. If the options really aren't clear, and the person can't seem to make a decision, you may see them eventually take up a position with just one shoulder raised – often with a comforting hand supporting the tilted head – as they struggle to come to a conclusion.

▼ Shoulder tension

You can tell tense shoulders because they are slightly raised, with the head shrinking just fractionally into the shoulders. This sign is a toned-down version of the ducking movement humans use when actually frightened by something, flinching away from a blow or a word, shoulders coming up to meet the ears as if to block off any sound.

Shoulder tension such as this can be a sign of many things. Combined with a wide, wary gaze it shows you that a person is anxious about something that may happen here and now; that they are actively watching and listening for the real-life problem to occur.

Alternatively, when someone has a defocused gaze, it's more likely that they're worried about something more general in their life, rather than something that is pressing in the here and now; the defocused gaze shows that they're thinking about the problem, while the shoulder tension indicates their reaction to the train of thought. You'll see that some natural worriers have a consistently stressed posture, which includes permanently raised shoulders.

When used in conjunction with an averted gaze, a turn-away or blocking hand or arm, raised shoulders can also signal to you that a person wants to be left alone – as mentioned earlier, this is truly the 'cold shoulder'. And, of course, if someone continuously prefers solitude – in other words, they are a natural introvert – then their natural posture will permanently include those protective, off-putting shoulders.

▶ ▲ Arms crossed

Crossed arms are often said to indicate a closed mind, but this interpretation is only one of many possible explanations. Admittedly, if you notice other signals of non-comprehension, such as a blank expression, a furrowed forehead, or a slight lean of the head, then arms folded across the body may well be a signal that a listener is not taking in what is happening.

Similarly if a person's shoulders are tensely raised, and there are minute head shakes, then there may well be underlying disagreement, with the arms performing a blocking function, as if to keep suggestions at bay. And if feelings escalate towards anger – shown by pursed lips, raised voice and lowered brow – then the crossed arms may

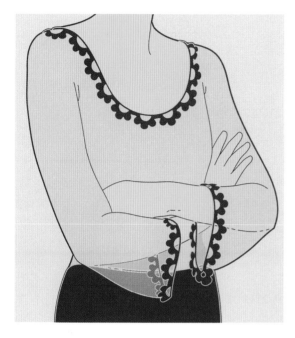
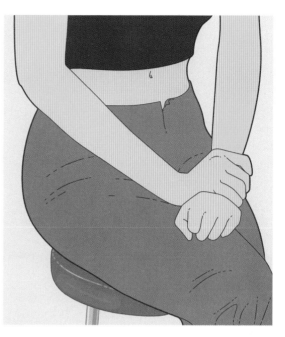

tense and pull into the side of the body with the hands unconsciously clenched into fists.

But folded arms can have other, much more innocuous intentions. They can be a shield: women use this signal more than men, perhaps because they are protecting their breasts.

Equally, if it's cold, a person will instinctively try to conserve heat by holding themselves around the middle – where the most vital organs are situated. And if leaning back in a chair for long periods, a person will often cross their arms in order to relax in a different position. In all these situations, you may, quite rightly, conclude that in fact they're not defending themselves against anything or anyone and that crossed arms are not a negative signal.

▶ ▲ Hand as a fist

A hand that is openly formed into a fist is a world-wide expression of aggression. Its meaning is obvious – 'I'm going to hit you …' – and its origins are clear. Primates clench their fists to hit each other in play or anger, and either back off or square up for a fight if this gesture is used to

them. It's usually accompanied by an angry or threatening expression, lowered eyebrows, a forward thrust of the lips, and a skin colour change as the body gets ready for action.

Most adults rarely use a clenched fist gesture to threaten violence seriously. What you may see them do, though, is to unconsciously clench their fists when they are angry or irritated. This 'slip of the hand', particularly when words and facial expression are gentle or placating, indicates someone's real feelings about the situation, feelings that are too socially threatening to be shown. Indeed, you may notice a person placing their other hand over the fist to hide it or 'hold down' the violent hand as if to stop taking action.

An obvious clenched fist also has other meanings world-wide. On the one hand, in many European countries, a clenched fist at the end of a bent and upward jerking arm is an insult, a crude reference to the sexual act. In Japan, on the other hand, a fist punched lightly into a person's stomach conveys the concept of suicide – reflecting the clenching of the fist around the ritual knife used in Japanese *seppuku*.

▲ Hand to head

When someone puts a hand to their head, they could be indicating a number of things. If the head is resting heavily on the hand, the person's head and eyes are angled downwards and their mouth pouts or turns down at the corners, you would be right to think that they are feeling unhappy or stressed. The supporting hand acts as a comforter; its touch will also literally be calming the person, lowering their heart rate and blood pressure, and reducing the adrenaline in their bloodstream. Any gentle, supportive touch – from oneself or from another trusted person – will achieve this physiological pacifying; for humans, as for animals, a gentle touch reminds us of the safety of childhood, and calms us down.

Equally, the hand-to-head position can show mental activity. It may signal concentration – if the whole body posture is alert, with raised head and direct eye gaze that follows what is happening; here, the support of the hand helps a person really focus on what is going around them. Hand to head may also be a sign that a person is sceptical or is having a mental discussion with themselves – if it combines with the sideways gaze and slightly tilted head that makes up the gesture known as the 'telephone position'.

▲ Hand over mouth

Placing the hand over the mouth is usually a sign that means the person is hiding something. This might be something literal and physical; in Western countries, at any rate, it is considered impolite to belch or hiccup with the mouth uncovered, or eat with the mouth open and the contents visible. So a person will slide their hand up to their mouth to stifle a tired yawn, or when they are removing pieces of inedible food from between their teeth.

In normal conversation, however, you may also see a person lift their hand to their mouth if they want to hide what they are saying or what they might say – it's a typically feminine signal.

A hand lifted to the mouth half-way through a sentence, accompanied by wide eyes and a slight flinch, usually means that the person has said something they didn't mean to and is now metaphorically wishing the words back into their mouth. A hand to mouth as someone carries on speaking, along with a lowered head and eyes and a mumbling voice, shows that the person feels they have to keep talking – maybe because it will seem suspicious if they don't – but doesn't really want you to hear or to believe what they are actually saying.

▲ Head angled

In primate tribes, tilting the head was a way of hearing more clearly, allowing the ear to have freer access to sounds that might signal approaching danger. The gesture is still a signal that someone is interested and involved and is a particularly feminine signal. As always, you have to interpret the precise meaning of the movement in terms of other body signals. If someone literally wants to hear more clearly, they will tend to lean forward as well as tilt their head slightly. If actual hearing is not the issue, but showing approval of a speaker is the aim, then you may see them remain quite still, smile slightly and nod or move in time with the speaker's words.

If a person wants to know more, then they will combine that head tilt with two seemingly contradictory signals – a frown and a smile – to show that they are confused or uncertain, but still approve of what is happening and want the speaker to carry on. In addition, if someone is upset or angry about what is being said, but still needs to carry on listening, then they will let that anger or sadness show in their eyes, eyebrows and mouth – or will blank their expression slightly so that their real feelings don't prevent the speaker from continuing.

A head tilt can also show you that someone is 'listening to themselves'. A person who is thinking about sounds, music or speech – or who is rehearsing a conversation or debating an important decision – will also tilt their head; this tilt can be combined with a hand-to-head gesture to form the 'telephone position'. People who do this a lot, whose intrinsic personality revolves around what they can hear, will often carry their head at a slight angle naturally and permanently.

▼ Eyes wide

The original function of wide-open eyes is obvious – to see better. But reasons for wanting to see better can vary. Perhaps someone's eyes open wide in pleasure, flying open in pleased surprise; if so, their mouth will slightly open too while their eyebrows will rise. You'll often see a toned-down version of this expression if a person is talking to someone they like or about something they like: their eyes will stay open slightly wider than usual over long periods of time. In fact, because wide eyes signal approval, they are an appealing body language signal and will create a strong positive response in others – which is why people open their eyes wider than normal when flirting, and why eye-widening makeup can make women seem more attractive.

Fascinatingly, human eyes will also open wide even when an attractive option isn't physically present. When a person is talking or listening,

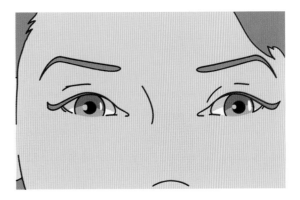

they will often mark, with a slight widening of their eyes, any spoken adjectives – words that describe things. They attempt to see better what they are visualizing in their mind's eye!

A wide stare can also, however, be a signal of unpleasant surprise. Often called 'flash-bulb eyes', a person's expression will be more fearful, their eyebrows drawing together as if to protect them from the unattractive sight. And if a person is angry, or in a confrontational mood, they often deliberately widen their eyes into a full stare, with heavily lowered eyebrows and lips aggressively pushed forward. This kind of gaze, originally a prelude to fighting behaviour, can by itself deter someone from doing something – as you may notice when watching an adult controlling a child by gaze alone. Studies have shown that just a steady stare of more than ten seconds creates anxiety and discomfort in a subordinate – although such a stare can make equals or superiors respond aggressively, so leading to a fight.

▶ ▲ Raised eyebrows

The eyebrow 'flash' – rapid raising of the eyebrows for about a sixth of a second – is a basic surprise signal. A person's eyes will fly wide open to see what is happening, while their eyebrows rise momentarily to make seeing easier. This movement has also developed a social meaning, observed in monkeys as well as in humans, of catching the attention of another person, or letting them know they're being looked at. It's almost as if we humans appear slightly surprised in order to signal to someone else that there is a reason for surprise: our meeting them.

The eyebrow flash is a world-wide human signal of acknowledgement, indicating welcome and appreciation; societies as far apart as the Balinese and the Bushmen show the same signal with the same meaning. You'll see people eyebrow-flash instinctively when they meet someone they like or want to get to know – and

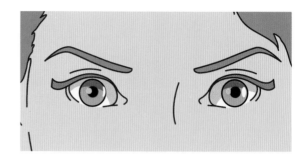

then repeat the movement continuously throughout an interaction with someone they want to impress or flirt with.

There are other meanings for raised eyebrows, however. When the movement is carried out slowly, over a few seconds, along with a tilted head, it usually comes at the end of a sentence, as a check on whether the listener has understood. When the movement occurs even more slowly, with a lift of the head, it can signal disapproval, a statement that 'I am surprised – at you, for your behaviour'. And with the lowering of the head and eyelids, particularly with pursed lips and a slight turn away, raised eyebrows take disapproval much further, signalling 'I want to cut off contact, and stop communicating with you entirely'.

▶ ▲ Pupil dilation

Many physical stimuli cause human pupils to dilate. Certain drugs do so, as does physical effort such as tightening muscles in the body. Eyes that are closed and then sharply opened display pupils that are larger, until they adjust to the light. Anticipation of a loud noise can make pupils enlarge – almost as if the expected shock creates a desire to check out our surroundings thoroughly.

Perhaps the most fascinating reasons why pupils dilate are not physical, however, but mental. Studies have shown that if a person is emotionally aroused by what they see, their pupils dilate to allow them to see more; this can be that they are attracted to a sight, or that they are sufficiently wary of it to want to know more.

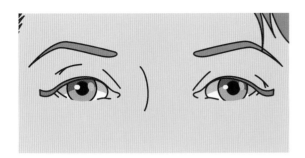
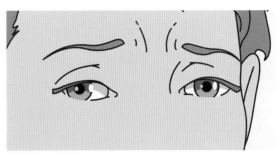

The message that pupil size sends to others is whether they are arousing to the watcher or not. Obviously, others are going to react more positively if they sense, through pupil size in the context of other positive signals, that the watcher finds them appealing; hence pupil dilation flatters and so attracts others. This is why, centuries ago, Italian women employed the drug belladonna ('beautiful lady') to enlarge artificially their pupils and make them seem more beautiful. Unless you do use such artificial stimulants it isn't possible to consciously control pupil size. Therefore, if a person is genuinely attracted to someone else, there is no way they can hide their pupil response. If they are not attracted the signals they send will be neutral or negative.

▶ ▲ Forehead raised

A slightly raised forehead, with slight lines across it, is often a sign that someone is thinking about something they've seen; they are thinking visually.

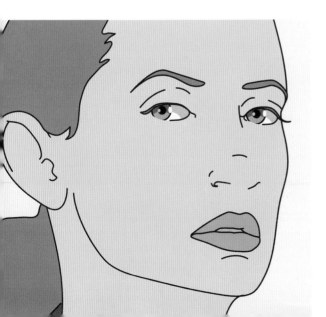

The raising movement can happen momentarily, is gone almost before it's noticed, and is usually accompanied by a slight uplift of the eyes. A person who thinks in visual terms a great deal often has permanent forehead wrinkles much earlier than normal ageing would create, even when the rest of the face is unlined.

If you see forehead raising lasting a second or two it's usually a sign of some strong emotion. Studies done by Paul Ekman in 1979 show that someone feeling sad will raise their eyebrows as if to let the tears flow more easily, and so create noticeable lines in the centre of the forehead. Obviously to interpret fully any forehead movement you have to look at other facial signals, particularly of the eyes and mouth, which by their angle, position and movement will show which of the emotions someone is experiencing.

The figure in the illustration above shows a mixture of surprise, anxiety and sadness in her face – as if she had just heard bad news.

◀ Nostrils flaring

Nostrils, the organs of smell, open and close in response to odour. So flaring nostrils can mean that a person smells something good such as food and wants more of it, or alternatively senses something dangerous such as poison and is alerted to that danger. Nostrils widen automatically in response to ammonia – and, in fact, even if dangerous substances are simply talked about, human noses can instinctively respond in the same way.

Nostrils also widen to let in more air, which allows the body to prepare for action more easily – another response to peril. And so primates use the nostril flare as a threat sign, a signal to other animals that they are ready to attack, a signal to other tribal members that they are threatened enough to need support. In humans, emotional threat produces the same reaction. If angry or irritated, a person's nostrils flare outwards to indicate that something is wrong and they feel bad about it.

▼ Pursed lips

Lip movements provide some of the most trustworthy bodytalk signals because they're the most unconscious. If someone purses their lips, then they make their mouth look like a purse, which, of course, was originally a draw-string bag. Firstly, a person will purse their mouth for a kiss, particularly one given or received from a friend with whom they're not sexually intimate, and from whom they therefore won't be expecting an open-mouthed kiss.

Combined with body closeness, movements that invite contact and the half-closed eyes that signal physical trust, a 'pucker' is an obvious sign that a social kiss is expected.

But someone will also purse their lips if they have a decision to make and are thinking things through. Then, you may see that their lips move slightly as they purse them, almost as though they are chewing over the alternatives. They may accompany this with all the typical signs of decision-making, such as a 'weighing' movement of hands or shoulders or a sideways head tilt. As soon as the decision is made, the lip movement stops and the mouth returns to its normal shape.

And someone may purse their lips in disapproval. The other body signs reflect this: the person will draw back slightly, look down their nose, raise their eyebrows, shake their head slowly (in a very different movement from the decision-tilt that accompanies thoughtfully pursed lips). They may breathe in deeply through the nose, expand the rib cage and then let the breath out sharply and noisily. They are most definitely not amused.

▼ Curled lips

The curled lips of a true sneer show the teeth. In primates, this indicates that, if necessary, they will use their teeth to fight. In humans, it indicates antagonism towards someone else – either simply through disapproval or because of anger or disgust.

Some sneering because of disgust gives a wrinkling movement of the nose along with the curl of the lip. The lower eyelid is pulled up as if to shut out the revolting sight, and the person may pull back involuntarily, or tilt their head back as if repelled by what they are experiencing.

In an angry sneer, however, a person will open their eyes wide and jut their face forward as if to confront an intruder. Their nostrils flare threateningly and their whole body tenses ready for action.

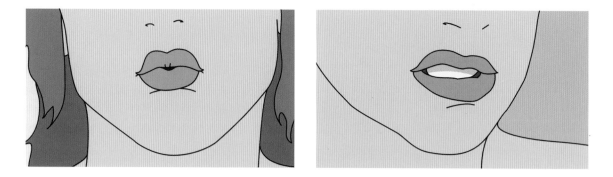

Most sneers, in fact, combine elements of both disgust and anger, so you may see a combination of the two emotions in the body language.

Sometimes, a person will curl their lips as they smile, the corners of their mouth rising at the same time as the centre of their upper lip wrinkles. While others may smile genuinely at something, the person with the curled lip doesn't find it funny. They are forcing a positive response – but other more negative emotions also come through, turning the attempt into a wry smile.

▲ Wide smile

Any smile is, at least on the surface, a positive sign. Primates smile when they are unthreatened. Humans smile when happy. The mouth curves, the corners tilt upwards equally, the lips may open wide to show the teeth in an unthreatening way.

The eyes wrinkle using the orbicularis oculi (the muscle that gives you crows' feet), while the skin colour often changes as the body relaxes.

You'll only sometimes spot this genuine smile, however. People are often expected to smile when not genuinely happy, to reassure people or show social approval. Women in particular smile whatever is happening.

If a smile is not genuine, a person will often show you various emotional signals creeping in from other parts of their face. The muscles surrounding the eyes won't wrinkle; instead, irritation will cause the person to stare slightly or wariness will cause them to shift their gaze sideways. Anger may flare the nostrils or disgust tighten the jaw. And a false smile will last longer than a genuine one and fade more slowly – as if trying to convince someone that it's for real.

▼ Legs crossed

There are many ways for someone to cross their legs. Crossing legs at the knee with toes relaxed is the commonest option for women, though a rare one for men to use; in some cultures, a man taking up that position may even have his masculinity called into question. Stretching out legs and crossing them at the knee emphasizes length, slimness and beauty, while placing a hand lengthways down the leg also draws attention to it; you'll see these movements most usually used by women when a prospective partner is in the room.

Crossing legs at the ankle is less feminine than crossing at the knee, and may be used by both genders; stretching out in this situation gives a casual air to a person's position, particularly if they lean back in their chair. Tilting the feet back or circling a foot is very informal, usually only done when with friends or family.

Crossing one leg at the knee and resting it across the other leg is a very masculine posture; women hardly ever use it and usually only when they are relaxed and wearing trousers. It is also a very confident position, taking up a great deal of

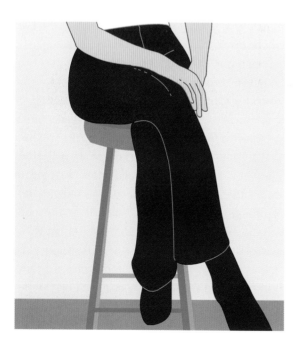

space and often showing that the person is sure of themselves and of their place in the group.

A final interesting aspect of crossed legs is where they point. The direction of the upper leg and foot can, in context, show what a person is interested in. If a discussion is taking place, these body parts will often point in the direction of whoever is speaking. If the focus of a discussion switches, they will often swing to point out whoever takes the floor. And if an argument is taking place, often you'll see one foot swinging slightly but continuously, from one speaker to the other.

▶ Legs wide

Sitting with legs wide apart is a comfortable position. Many people will sit like this when they feel safe or unobserved; at a dinner party, when legs are hidden by the table cloth, men and women will sit like this in more or less equal numbers. But 'legs apart' is also a very vulnerable position. Unless they feel they are physically and emotionally safe, both genders instinctively keep their genitals protected and hidden, by closing their legs completely or crossing them at the ankle or knee. When asked to sit with legs open in public, most people will try to 'defend' themselves by placing papers on their lap, or sliding their hands down to mask their genitals.

Because of its vulnerability, legs apart is a position most people adopt only with friends or family. You can often tell how relaxed a group is by the number who are sitting with their legs wide apart – few people would spread their legs wide at an important business meeting, or when with someone they are just getting to know.

Finally, legs apart is a very confident position, often used by those who are the leaders in a group, by men rather than women, by younger rather than older people. It takes up space, forcing others to give way. It keeps a person balanced and appearing steady in a way that the 'legs-crossed' posture doesn't.

draw attention to it, or curling away as if to avoid it (of course, feet will also 'point' to someone or something that is particularly attractive, so causing positive bodily tension). And feet can indicate dominance; someone who regards themselves as superior in an interaction will point their feet outwards, while someone who feels inferior will point their feet inwards.

Feet will also betray emotion when what someone is feeling is irritation or anger rather than nervousness or anxiety. Then, their feet are likely to be solidly tense, pressed against each other, or moving with tiny, sharp, focused kicks rather than nervous wriggles. Happy feet, conversely, are either excited – wriggling as if nervous, but rhythmically and with energy – or contented – relaxedly stretching and curling.

It may not be going too far to suggest that, when trying to understand someone through body language, you should perhaps start at the feet and work up.

▶ Feet curled

Because the feet, of all human body parts, are the furthest away from the face, people instinctively, and often correctly, believe that their feet are not watched by other people. So when all someone's energy is put into hiding their emotions as revealed in their facial expression or hand gestures you may still be able to spot their true feelings revealed through their feet.

Tense feet often signify anxiety or nervousness. They wind around each other, or around the furniture, for the comfort of touch. They stretch and curl to release their tension. They will often wriggle, or kick, in 'escape movements' that show a desire to be away from a worrying situation. Foot tension is particularly likely to occur when someone is in a situation such as an interview where they feel they have to stay put.

In addition, feet, like hands and legs, can also indicate the source of the tension – pointing to

index

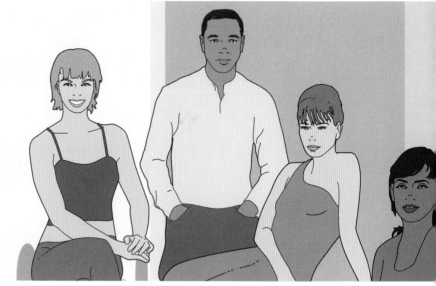

Acknowledgements

My thanks to everyone who
has helped with this book,
particularly Lisa Dyer, Zoe Dissell
and all the staff at Carlton
Books; Robin Max Marder; my
agent Barbara Levy; my support
team of Charlie Ham, Gaia Fleet
and Colin Marsh. A special
thank you to my husband Ian
who as always makes even the
impossible possible.